3-MINUTE DEVOTIONS FOR BOYS AGES 10-12

DAILY DEVOTIONAL FOR BOYS

ANDERS BENNETT

ADISAN Publishing AB

INTRODUCTION

Have you ever taken a long road trip with your family? There are parts of that trip that are wonderful, right? It's great to see new things and experience new places. It can be fun to make up new games as you ride down the road or listen to good music. But we can be honest about one thing about road trips; they can be boring.

Eventually, you run out of music to listen to. Your siblings may start to annoy you. And the trees whizzing by your window all begin to look the same. Sometimes, even short road trips can feel incredibly long and drawn out.

I would take a road trip with my family to my grandma's house every year for Christmas. I loved going there because she made the best buttermilk biscuits you've ever had. And we always played a lot of board games together. It was great! But we had to drive from North Carolina to South Carolina. That doesn't look far on a map, but trust me. It was a long ride.

Even better than the trip to grandma's, as much fun as it was, was when we got home. There is just something special about coming home after being gone for a long time. Have you ever noticed that your house has a special smell? Go on a trip for a week, and you'll notice it when you come home. It smells like comfort. It smells like relaxation. It smells like home.

Did you know that the Bible tells us that we are all on a long journey? It's almost like we are on a road trip. The Bible says that we are travelers and that this world is not our home. No, we are not Martians from space. But there is a place for everyone after they die. For Christians, this place is called Heaven. A good name for it would be "Home." Since we are called travelers here, then home must be there. It's the place where we can finally kick our feet up on the couch and rest.

The Bible is like our road map on this long journey home. It tells us where to go and how to get there. It tells us what life will be like when we get to Heaven. But most of the Bible is there to tell us how to navigate the world we live in now. It's a book for travelers.

This is why, for the next year, we will be reading this book together. Each week, we will study one verse from the Bible and think about how it helps us on our long journey home. Even when we have a full year to study, we won't read the whole Bible. We're going to focus on a very important story that takes up about 7 books of the Bible. It's the story of how God's people went on a long journey to their new home called The Promised Land and their journey of development until they reached the reign of King David.

We will learn a lot along the way. We will learn how good God is and how reliable He can be. We will learn how selfish we can be sometimes when we are in scary and hard situations. And, wonderfully, we will learn how forgiving God can be when we act so selfishly. You see, if there's one big thing to learn from the Bible, it's that God loves you. Over and over again, He tells us that. And so, over the course of this year, if you ever feel lost, pull out your road map. Open up the Bible and be reminded that God loves you and welcomes you on this long journey home.

HOW-TO-USE

This book is to help Preteens like you learn how to make it on your long journey home. It has three parts to it. There is a daily Bible verse. There is a short explanation of what that verse means and why it's important. And there is a reflection question to help you think about how that verse can change your day.

Each of these parts is important for you to get the most out of the book. If you've ever tried squeezing toothpaste out of a toothpaste container, then you'll know what I mean. If you put just a little bit of effort in, then you'll get most of the toothpaste out. But if you work hard and squeeze as much as you can, you'll find that there is more to get.

The same is true with this book and with the Bible. If you take your time and work hard at understanding each page, then you'll get a lot more out of it. If you try to go through it too quickly, you'll get something, but not all there is for you. This is why you need to decide when you want to read this book.

If you have a certain time each day that you read this book, you'll be able to take your time with it, and you'll do it more often. If you just wait until the end of the day or when you have some free time, you probably won't. Between homework, sports, and playing with your family, there is not much free time.

So, before you read any more, decide when you want to read each day. Seriously, put the book down and talk with your parents. Decide when you want to read. Have you decided yet? Good. Now hand your book to your parents or grandparents for this next part.

A NOTE TO PARENTS

Dear parents, your preteen is about to start a very important and meaningful walk through the Scriptures. If I've done my job right, they will want to talk with you about what they are reading. They are going to have questions that I don't have time to answer in this book. This is where I need your help. Better yet, this is where your preteen needs your help.

Deuteronomy 6:4-9 says, "Hear, O Israel: The Lord our God, the Lord is one. You shall love the Lord your God with all your heart and with all your soul and with all your might. And these words that I command you today shall be on your heart. You shall teach them diligently to your children and shall talk of them when you sit in your house, when you walk by the way, when you lie down, and when you rise. You shall bind them as a sign on your hand, and they shall be as frontlets between your eyes. You shall write them on the doorposts of your house and on your gates."

The Bible is clear that it is our job as parents to help our children know Jesus. This book is a great tool for you to do that job. Each day, they will read about a different story in the Bible. They will have a question at the end of each day that will help them reflect on the story. Use that question as a conversation starter. Dig into God's Word with them to help them understand. You may find that you end up learning just as much as they do. Praise the Lord if that's the case.

The most important thing you can do now is pray. Pray for your child. Pray for the Holy Spirit to begin softening their hearts. Pray that God will "open [their] eyes, that [they] may behold wondrous things out of [His] law." Now, hand this book back to your child. They have work to do!

*But the people of Israel were fruitful and increased greatly; they
multiplied and grew exceedingly strong, so that the land was
filled with them.*

Exodus 1:7

The Bible is a huge book. It is one huge book made up of 66 little books inside. That could be overwhelming to think about and to try to understand. But if you think of the Bible as one big story, it helps to make sense of it all. So let me tell you what that one big story is all about.

The big story of the Bible is all about God's people. It is about how God plans to save his people. In the book of Exodus, our verse from today, God's people are called Israel. At the beginning of this book, Israel is growing in size and in strength. That all began with one person named Abraham growing from his little family of three to thousands of people in the country of Egypt.

What makes a good story?

*But the more they were oppressed, the more they multiplied
and the more they spread abroad. And the Egyptians
were in dread of the people of Israel.*

Exodus 1:12

Have you ever spent the night at a friend's house? Those nights can be a lot of fun with a lot of exciting things. You can play fun new games and eat yummy food. But there are also new rules and expectations which can be hard to learn and follow. Imagine going over to a friend's house and having a terrible time. Imagine never being able to leave that person's house even though you desperately want to go home.

This is what the book of Exodus is all about. God's people are slaves in Egypt. They desperately want to go home. But they can't seem to find a way out. But God has not left them alone. Even through the painful times that they experience in Egypt, he allows them to grow and become stronger. He is preparing them for the day when he will lead them back home.

Why did God's people want to go home?

*But the midwives feared God and did not do as the king of Egypt
commanded them, but let the male children live.*

Exodus 1:17

The king of Egypt was called the Pharaoh. And the pharaoh that was in charge during this day was evil and mean. He did not like that God's people were growing in size and in strength. And so he put together a wicked plan to weaken God's people. His wicked plan was to have every little boy that was born thrown into the Nile River.

But God's people would not do that. The midwives (those were the ladies who took care of babies) hid all the little boys when they were born. They risked their own lives to save the lives of others. They were brave women. It makes me wonder if I would be as brave as them if I had to do what they did. What do you think?

Can you think of a time when God helped you be brave?

*When she could hide him no longer, she took for him a basket
made of bulrushes and daubed it with bitumen and pitch. She put
the child in it and placed it among the reeds by the river bank.*

Exodus 2:3

One of the little boys who was born that day was named Moses. Moses's mom loved him so much when he was born that she did what the midwives were doing. She hid her little boy. The only way she could think of doing this was to put him in a waterproof basket and set him in the reeds in the river. The idea was that if he stayed in the reeds, he would not float down the river.

Unfortunately, the basket carrying her little boy floats away. Moses' big sister ran down the river to keep watch over him and to make sure that he was safe. The basket stopped in front of Pharaoh's house. But it was not Pharaoh who walked outside and found it. It was Pharaoh's daughter. What will happen to baby Moses?

Have you ever had to watch out for someone?

When the child grew older, she brought him to Pharaoh's daughter,
and he became her son. She named him Moses, "Because,"
she said, "I drew him out of the water."
Exodus 2:10

Pharaoh's daughter saved baby Moses. When she saw him in the basket in the river, she had compassion for him. She wanted to take care of him and make sure that he was safe. And God did an amazing thing that day. Do you remember that Moses's sister was watching over him? She came out from her hiding place and told Pharaoh's daughter that she knew someone who could take care of Moses until he was older.

So Pharaoh's daughter said that she could take the baby. Do you know who Moses's sister knew? It was his mom. What an incredible thing! God worked it out so that even when Moses' mom gave him up to be protected by God in the river, she was able to get him back.

How has God kept you safe?

One day, when Moses had grown up, he went out to his people and looked on their
burdens, and he saw an Egyptian beating a Hebrew, one of his people.
Exodus 2:11

After Moses's mom had raised him for a few years, she had to give him back to the Pharaoh's daughter. And Moses grew up in Pharaoh's house. He was raised like any other Egyptian boy. He went to an Egyptian school and learned to play Egyptian games. But when Moses was older, he realized that he didn't know much about Israel. He did not know God's people very well.

That bothered him because he was an Israelite. He was supposed to be one of God's people. So he ventured out of Pharaoh's Palace one day to see how the Israelites were doing. But he was so sad at what he saw. He was angry, too. They were not being treated fairly. And Moses wanted to step in and save them. But the way he tried to help was wrong. He killed an Egyptian man and tried to hide what he did.

When have you stood up for someone being hurt?

10

*The shepherds came and drove them away, but Moses stood
up and saved them, and watered their flock.*
Exodus 2:17

I love to watch movies. Do you? Have you ever learned about how movies are made? Whenever they are using a camera to make a movie, they have to take multiple shots. And before each time they film a scene, they say, "Take one" or "Take two," depending on how many times they have shot that scene. This verse is like Moses saying, "Take two."

Do you remember what he did the last time he saw someone in trouble? He killed someone to save them. That was not the right thing to do. But this time, he sees some more people in trouble. Instead of killing someone, he protects someone. He saves someone without taking someone else's life. Moses is learning what it means to be a protector. But he still has a lot of questions about how he can help God's people.

Why does God want us to protect others?

*She gave birth to a son, and he called his name Gershom,
for he said, "I have been a sojourner in a foreign land."*
Exodus 2:22

Moses was a shepherd for most of his life. As a boy, he was raised in an Egyptian home. And now, as an adult, he has lived his life on a farm, taking care of sheep. Although he had a wife, and they had just had a baby boy of their own, Moses still did not feel like he was home. He named his boy as a reminder to himself that he was still a stranger in a foreign land.

The old heartache of wanting to know God's people came back. So Moses began to try to figure out a way to save God's people and feel like he was home at last. Moses did not know what to do. He did not know how to help. But Moses was not alone. Whether he was in a basket in the river, in Pharaoh's house, or in the middle of a pasture, God was with him.

Can you think of a time when God was with you?

And God heard their groaning, and God remembered his
covenant with Abraham, with Isaac, and with Jacob.
Exodus 2:24

This verse has two of the most important things you need to know about God. It teaches us that God hears and that God remembers. It is important to know that God hears because if we are ever in trouble, we can know for sure that God is listening. No matter how far away we feel like he is or how alone we feel like we are, God is always listening.

And God always remembers. God made a promise to Abraham a long, long time ago that he would never leave his people alone. And so, when God's people called out for help, he heard them, and he remembered the prom he made to them. And God has never failed to keep his promise. This means that God keeps the same promise to you. If you ever feel alone, remember that God will never leave you.

How does this verse make you feel?

Then he said, "Do not come near; take your sandals off your feet,
for the place on which you are standing is holy ground."
Exodus 3:5

In the middle of a sheep pasture, God spoke to Moses. And he did it in a really strange way. Moses looked around and saw a bush that had caught on fire. And if that wasn't strange enough, the bush wasn't burning. No matter how hot the fire got, the sticks and the leaves were not burning away.

So Moses went closer to see what was going on, and that is when God spoke to him. And God said to him to take off his sandals because he was on holy ground. This means that he was in a very special place. He was in the presence of God. God did not want anything, even Moses' sandals, to stand in the way of being as close as possible to Him. Moses could feel the warmth of the fire and be reminded how warm and close God was to him.

What is the most special place you've ever been to?

Come, I will send you to Pharaoh that you may bring
my people, the children of Israel, out of Egypt."
Exodus 3:10

God has heard the prayers of his people. He will not let them experience the hardship. They are facing no longer. Out of everyone that God could've chosen to deliver his people from Egypt, he uses the most unlikely person. He used the little boy that should not have lived. He uses an Israelite who was raised as an Egyptian. He uses the man who murdered him and ran away. He uses an 80-year-old shepherd.

This is how God works. He uses unlikely people to do unlikely things. By doing this, he gets the most glory for it. Because how else can you explain a deliverer being successful like this? Who else could get the credit for delivering Israel from slavery in Egypt? It can only be God, and that's how he likes it.

Where else in the Bible has God used an unlikely person?

But Moses said to God, "Who am I that I should go to Pharaoh
and bring the children of Israel out of Egypt?"
Exodus 3:11

When Moses is given the task of saving God's people from the hands of Egypt, he is scared. He asks, "Who am I that I should go?" In other words, he is trying to figure out what makes him so special. Moses knows his background. He knows that he has made big mistakes. And he knows his limitations. And yet God has called him to go back to Egypt.

We live a life because God requires us to trust him. This means that when he asks us to do things that are scary and hard, we still follow him. Even if it doesn't make sense in our minds, we still trust him. If God is who he says he is, then his way is always going to be the best.

What is a hard thing God asks you to do?

*God said to Moses, "I am who I am." And he said, "Say this
to the people of Israel: 'I am has sent me to you.'"*
Exodus 3:14

When Moses talks to God about his fears, God gives him an answer. Moses wants to know, "What am I supposed to say when I get there?" He wants to know who he should say has sent him to Pharaoh. And God gives him a strange answer. God tells him to say, "I am has sent me." What does God mean?

This can be a tricky one. But think about it with me for just a minute. God does not say, "I was." God does not say, "I will be." God says, "I am." What he means is that He is the everlasting God. There will never be a moment where he is not there. He is the Great I Am.

How does this give you comfort today?

*So I will stretch out my hand and strike Egypt with all the
wonders that I will do in it; after that he will let you go.*
Exodus 3:20

Moses had a lot of questions about how this would all work. And so God graciously gave him the game plan. If you play sports, you know that your coaches always have a game plan in mind. They want each player to do the right thing at the right time so they can win the game. God has a game plan for Moses. And it has two parts.

First, God says that he will stretch out his hand and strike Egypt with wonders. This means that God is going to do something miraculous that is going to cause pain to the Egyptians. The second part is that Pharaoh will let them go. This is a promise that God makes. Once they see how powerful he is, they will let his people go.

What is the most powerful thing God can do?

*And he said, "Throw it on the ground." So he threw it on the
ground, and it became a serpent, and Moses ran from it.*
Exodus 4:3

God told Moses what to say. God told him what was going to happen. And Moses was still scared. So Moses asked for a sign that he could show to the Pharaoh to prove that he was from God. And so God gave him a couple of signs. One of them was the ability to turn his staff into a snake and then back into a staff again.

The way that it would work is when Moses would throw his staff on the ground. It would turn into a snake. And then, when he reached to pick it back up, it would turn into a staff again. If Moses could perform this miracle, Pharaoh would have to believe that he was from God. Who else could turn a staff into a snake?

What other miracles has God done in the Bible?

*But Moses said to the Lord, "Oh, my Lord, I am not eloquent,
either in the past or since you have spoken to your servant, but I
am slow of speech and of tongue."*
Exodus 4:10

Have you ever been tongue-tied? I know that I have. It can be frustrating and embarrassing to fumble through your words. Moses was not a very good speaker. We don't know exactly what the problem was. But it may be that he had a stutter. He was worried that he couldn't lead people because he had a stutter. So Moses told God about what he was worried about.

God encouraged Moses and let him know that he would be with him no matter what. Whatever speech issue Moses had would not be enough to drive God away or to prevent him from being used. Moses still left discouraged. So, God began working on a plan to help Moses overcome those fears.

Do you have trouble doing something that God can help with?

DAY 17: BACK TO EGYPT

*So Moses took his wife and his sons and had them ride on a
donkey, and went back to the land of Egypt. And Moses
took the staff of God in his hand.*
Exodus 4:20

This was a big moment for Moses. He was finally going back to Egypt. Do you remember why he ran away to begin with? Moses murdered an Egyptian. He was caught by an Israelite. And so he ran away. It's been a long time since Moses has gone back home. But because God was calling him to return, he did.

I can imagine this was a nerve-wracking moment. Moses hadn't seen his mom or his sister since he left. He hadn't seen his adoptive mom and family either. Pharaoh, Moses' grandpa, was the one who he had to go see. There were a lot of reasons for Moses to turn around. But He trusted God and returned.

When was the last time you had to do something scary?

DAY 18: HELP IS ON THE WAY

*Aaron spoke all the words that the Lord had spoken to Moses
and did the signs in the sight of the people.*
Exodus 4:30

Do you remember what Moses was worried about? He told God that he was worried he couldn't lead his people because he wasn't good at talking. I told you back then that God was already working on a plan to help him. Meet the plan. His name is Aaron. Did you notice what it says Aaron could do? Aaron spoke all the words that the Lord spoke.

The very thing that Moses was worried about being able to do, Aaron could do without any problems. Help was on the way for Moses. Aaron joined Moses and his family on their trip back to Egypt. What a kind God Moses has. What a kind God we have as well. When we need help, God is there for us. It may not be in the way we expect, but God is always present in our time of need.

When was a time when God helped you?

*Afterward Moses and Aaron went and said to Pharaoh,
"Thus says the Lord, the God of Israel, 'Let my people go,
that they may hold a feast to me in the wilderness.'"*
Exodus 5:1

Have you ever had to stand up to a bully? Maybe they were picking on you or one of your friends? That can be a hard thing to do. In this situation, Moses had to stand up to the meanest bully you can imagine. And to make things worse, it was the Pharaoh of Egypt. And to make it even harder, it was his grandpa. Can you imagine having to stand up to your grandpa?

Moses and Aaron entered Pharaoh's court that day and demanded what the Lord demanded. They said to let God's people go. And Pharaoh quickly said, "No!" They were Pharaoh's slaves. He couldn't afford to lose them. So, he refused to let God's people go over and over again.

Have you ever had to stand up to a bully?

*Then Moses turned to the Lord and said, "O Lord, why have you
done evil to this people? Why did you ever send me?*
Exodus 5:22

There is an old saying that goes like this: you have to break a few eggs to make an omelet. What that means is that sometimes things have to get worse before they get better. You have to make a mess before you can clean up. Well, things were getting worse for God's people. When Moses told Pharaoh to let God's people go, Pharaoh got mad.

He got so mad that he made God's people work harder than they ever had before. He made their lives miserable. Pharaoh wanted everyone to know that he was in control, not God. This upset Moses, which is why he asked, "Why did you ever send me?" But God had a plan. He had already told Moses. Things had to get worse before they could get better.

Have you ever had things get worse before they get better?

*But the Lord said to Moses, "Now you shall see what I will do to
Pharaoh; for with a strong hand he will send them out, and with
a strong hand he will drive them out of his land."*
Exodus 6:1

If you have ever been to see a movie at a movie theatre, then you know the anticipation of the previews. All the previews of upcoming movies only whet your appetite for the movie you came to see. And then the wonderful moment happened. The lights go dim. The screen rolls back. The sound is turned up. And the movie finally begins.

Consider this verse, the lights are going dim in Moses' life. God had already promised that He would use a strong hand to save His people from Pharaoh. And now, the time has come for the movie to begin. All the pieces are getting into place. It can be wonderful and exciting to see God working in our lives.

How has God worked in your life?

*I will take you to be my people, and I will be your God, and you
shall know that I am the Lord your God, who has brought you out
from under the burdens of the Egyptians.*
Exodus 6:7

Why would God go through all of this work to save the Israelites? What was His goal? He had one primary goal in mind. God wants to get the glory or worship that He deserves. To do that, He wants to be the God of all people. So, when He planned to save the Israelites, it was to show them that He alone was worthy of their praise.

He was graciously reaching out to them with a promise. He promised that He would save them and be their God forever. They did not have to do anything to earn that promise. It was not on their shoulders to keep the promise. God gave them what they hadn't earned. We call that grace.

How would you define grace?

*And the Lord said to Moses, "See, I have made you like God to
Pharaoh, and your brother Aaron shall be your prophet.*

Exodus 7:1

In the days of kings, knights, and jesters, there was a person called the town crier. His whole job was to stand in the middle of the town and cry out the decree of the king. When you watch movies or read books about this, it usually begins with, "Hear ye! Hear ye!" The town crier had a message from the king that he was to proclaim until everyone heard it.

The prophets in the Bible have the same job. Only their king is not someone sitting in a castle somewhere. No, their king is God Himself. He is seated on His throne in Heaven. But He does have a message to proclaim to the world. In the Old Testament, He did this through the prophets. Do you remember Aaron, Moses' helper? He was officially deemed the prophet during this journey.

Would you want to be a prophet or preacher?

*Thus says the Lord, "By this you shall know that I am the Lord:
behold, with the staff that is in my hand I will strike the water
that is in the Nile, and it shall turn into blood.*

Exodus 7:17

Over the course of ten interactions, Moses is going to plead with Pharaoh to let God's people go. And ten different times, Pharaoh is going to say, "No." This is going to result in ten different punishments in the form of plagues. Each of them will slowly destroy Egypt and undermine Pharaoh.

The first plague aims at the central point of Egypt, the Nile River. This was terrible for Egypt because when the river turned to blood, all the fish died. This meant that fishermen had no fish to catch. Families had no fish to eat. The city had no water to drink. It was devastating, but it did not change Pharaoh's mind.

Why would God start by turning the Nile to blood?

*But if you refuse to let them go, behold, I will plague all your
country with frogs.*
Exodus 8:2

As a kid, I used to think the second plague was silly. God promised to send frogs all across the land if Pharaoh didn't let His people go. Can you imagine that madness? Frogs are everywhere in sight. Frogs in your shoes, soup, and streets. It would be hilarious at first. But then it would be horrible.

What if everywhere you looked and everywhere you went, you couldn't escape frogs? The slimy feeling they leave, mixed with the constant ribbits, would drive you mad. Not to mention the diseases they carry and would spread all around town. With the river turned to blood, they would have nowhere to go but into the people's homes.

What would you do if your house was covered in frogs?

*Then the Lord said to Moses, "Say to Aaron, 'Stretch out your
staff and strike the dust of the earth, so that it may become gnats
in all the land of Egypt.'"*
Exodus 8:16

I love a lot of things about summer. The way the heat of the day is relieved by diving into a cool pool. Ice cream and lemonade after playing outside is an incredible treat. But there is one thing about summer that I cannot stand. Bugs are out in full force. Mosquitoes, flies, and gnats can look like clouds at times around a stagnant pool of water.

This was the third plague that God sent into Egypt in response to Pharaoh's defiance. Gnats covered the city as much as sand covered the ground. And remember, they were in the desert! There was plenty of sand to go around. If you thought frogs were bad, imagine this. The frogs would have been even more active in trying to catch all of these gnats. Egypt was quickly becoming a place where you could never feel clean or at ease.

How does being dirty for a long time make you feel?

Or else, if you will not let my people go, behold, I will send swarms of flies on you and your servants and your people, and into your houses. And the houses of the Egyptians shall be filled with swarms of flies, and also the ground on which they stand.

Exodus 8:21

Have your parents ever told you not to make them repeat themselves? Like when they have told you to clean your room, but you haven't even started yet. Well, I feel like God has repeated himself quite a bit with the Egyptians. The king of Egypt, called Pharaoh, did not want to listen to what God had to say. And so, God rightly continued to bring about punishment.

And the purpose of punishment is to help the punished learn to do what is right.

You see, in all of this God just wanted Egypt to see him as the one true God to worship him. He had good and pure intentions. It was love that drove his actions even when his actions were hard to bear. Like a father disciplines a child, so God was disciplining Egypt for their good.

What is the purpose of discipline?

Then Pharaoh called Moses and Aaron and said,
"Go, sacrifice to your God within the land."
Exodus 8:25

Finally, Pharaoh had had enough. I guess all the frogs and flies had finally made him think twice about going against God. And so Pharaoh said that God's people could go out and worship him. However, notice that Pharaoh did not say that God's people could be let go forever.

This moment was short-lived in Pharaoh's life. Because just as he is about to let them go, he changes his mind. He tells them, "Just kidding. I want you to stay here and keep working for me." He tells him that they cannot go and worship their God, and they definitely cannot stop being his slaves. That small glimmer of hope did not last long. And so God had to continue to bring about discipline and judgment until Pharaoh would finally listen.

Why do you think Pharaoh changed his mind?

*Behold, the hand of the Lord will fall with a very severe plague
upon your livestock that are in the field, the horses, the donkeys,
the camels, the herds, and the flocks.*

Exodus 9:3

Did God miss? So far, He has done things that directly affect people. He has turned their water into blood, covered their homes with frogs, and filled their land with flies and gnats. But now He has a plague on the animals. Why would God do this?

If you think about it, God's plague on the animals hits the people, too. If all of the cows die, what will they eat, and where will they get their milk? If all the horses die, how would they travel? If all the camels die, how would they transport goods from city to city? They can't. Without their livestock, the people are in great danger. They will become desperate. That's what they need to be.

Why do people need to become desperate?

*It shall become fine dust over all the land of Egypt, and become boils breaking out
in sores on man and beast throughout all the land of Egypt.*

Exodus 9:9

Have you ever had chicken pox? The itchy feeling that you have with the little bumps all over your body is horrible. I remember when I had it, my parents made me take a bath in oatmeal. Even that didn't stop the itching for long. But the chicken pox would be nothing compared to the boils that now plagued the Egyptian people. Covered in painful sores, their lives were becoming miserable.

God's plagues are getting closer and closer to the heart. What could be avoided has now become unavoidable. Boils were covering every person and animal. You can't go anywhere without getting infected or spreading it to other people. They were now dangerous to themselves and to their families. This puts them in a difficult position. There was nothing they could do to escape the punishment of God except to let His people go.

What is the sickest you've ever been?

But for this purpose I have raised you up, to show you my power,
so that my name may be proclaimed in all the earth.
Exodus 9:16

Have you ever played a game called chess? It is a board game that has been around for a long time. It is made up of a lot of different characters, and the strongest character is the queen. But the most important character is the king. If you can take the other person, King, you have a checkmate. That means that you win.

In this verse, God is saying to Pharaoh, "Checkmate, I got you." You see, he had a bigger goal in mind than just sending plagues. He wanted to do more than just free his people. He wanted to show the whole world that he alone is the one true God. God knew that Farah would not let his people go. It's so God was setting himself up to be the hero of the story and of his people forever. Checkmate. He wins.

How does it make you feel that God always wins?

Behold, about this time tomorrow I will cause very heavy hail to fall, such
as never has been in Egypt from the day it was founded until now.
Exodus 9:18

There is an old children's song that goes like this; rain, rain, go away, come again another day. Perhaps you have sung that in a disappointed tone because rain has once again ruined your ability to go outside and play. Rain can even ruin pool parties and trips to the park. In this verse, we are told about something much worse than rain ruining a party. We are told about hail.

Hail is like really hard snow. It is large drops of frozen rain. And the hail that fell on Egypt that day had never been seen like it before. This probably means this plague was big, really big for Egypt, very close to the point of no return. And as we have already seen, we know that they will not return. Utter devastation is coming their way.

How would you react to giant hail falling?

For if you refuse to let my people go, behold,
tomorrow I will bring locusts into your country,
Exodus 10:4

I grew up in a house that had 10 apple trees in the front yard. It was really fun to be able to climb those trees and pick the little apples that grew on them. But there were many times when we were not the only ones in the yard with the trees. There were deer that liked to come and play, too. And the thing they wanted to do the most was to eat the apples off the tree. This was fun and sometimes funny as a kid. But for the Egyptians facing the locusts, this was a terrible nightmare.

Have you ever had a nightmare? They are horrible dreams that only end when you wake up. Many times, you will jolt awake in fear. The only way that this nightmare will end for Egypt is if they confess that the God of Israel is the only true God. But sadly, they will not do that. They will have to deal with locusts everywhere, eating all of their crops.

What is the best dream you've ever had?

Then the Lord said to Moses, "Stretch out your hand toward heaven, that there may
be darkness over the land of Egypt, a darkness to be felt."
Exodus 10:21

I'm scared of the dark. I admit it. I am a fully grown adult, and I am terrified of the dark. We have a nightlight in our house. And we say that they are for kids. But I will be honest with you, those nightlights are for me. I do not like it when it is dark, and I cannot see what might be lurking around the corner.

Darkness is all that Egypt will know until the plague ends. This was a particularly powerful moment for God. You see, the Egyptians worship a God who claims to be fully in control of the sun. So, when the God of the Israelites was able to cut the sun off and leave them in darkness. It was proof that he was the stronger God. The darkness was everywhere, that God was everywhere, and they could not escape his punishment.

Why do so many people fear the dark?

*And every firstborn in the land of Egypt shall die, from the firstborn of Pharaoh
who sits on his throne, even to the firstborn of the slave girl who is behind the
handmill, and all the firstborn of the cattle.*
Exodus 11:5

The Bible teaches us that the wages of sin are death. What that means is
the cost of disobeying God is your life. That's a scary thing, but it's the same
thing God told Adam and Eve in the Garden of Eden. Egypt had been sinning
and sinning and sinning. And now the final punishment was coming. Every
firstborn child would be killed in the night.

You might think that that punishment is pretty harsh. Let me remind you
of what has happened already. God gave them 9 chances. He has given them
9 warnings. And his final punishment is exactly what Pharaoh did to the Israelites. The reason Moses has his name is that Pharaoh wanted all the boys
thrown into the Nile River. After all is said and done, God was right and did
justice in his punishment.

Do you think it's fair that death is the punishment for sin?

DAY 36: SACRIFICE

*Then they shall take some of the blood and put it on the two
doorposts and the lintel of the houses in which they eat it.*
Exodus 12:7

There was a way for anyone to be saved on that terrifying night. Whether
you were an Egyptian or an Israelite, you could be saved. What you had to do
was pretty simple. You had to take your best sheep and offer it as a sacrifice
to God. You would eat the meat and paint the blood on the doorposts of your
house. This action showed God that you worshiped Him alone.

This was a way for something else to pay the price for sin. If the punishment for sin is death, the sheep would pay that price in your place. This story
tells us about a bigger story to come. God was going to send His Son, Jesus, to
die in the place of sinners. And all who place their trust in Him will be saved
from death.

Why would God provide a way to be saved?

*In this manner you shall eat it: with your belt fastened, your
sandals on your feet, and your staff in your hand. And you shall
eat it in haste. It is the Lord's Passover.*

Exodus 12:11

What's your favorite holiday? Mine is Thanksgiving because of all the wonderful food you get to eat. Everything from fried turkey to cranberry sauce to sweet potato pie. It's one of the greatest holidays of the year. For God's People, Passover became their favorite holiday. They called it the Passover because the angel of death would pass over every house with the blood of the sheep on the doorpost.

This first Passover wasn't filled with presents and jolly conversation. They ate a quick meal with traveling clothes on. If everything went according to plan, they would be leaving that night to escape the Pharaoh and his army. Whenever they celebrate this holiday in years to come, they will remember how God saved them from death.

How can holidays make you think about God?

DAY 38: THE WORST NIGHT

*And Pharaoh rose up in the night, he and all his servants and all
the Egyptians. And there was a great cry in Egypt, for there
was not a house where someone was not dead.*

Exodus 12:30

This verse makes me so sad. I don't even want to imagine it. But it happened. One night, all the firstborn children in Egypt died. One morning, every parent woke up to that terrible sight. The Bible says that there was a great cry in Egypt. Everyone was affected. Pharaoh's pride had finally caught up with him, and it cost him dearly.

We would be wise to realize that all of God's words are true. Just like the promise that we will be saved if we trust in Jesus, the promise that we will die for our sins is true, too. Proverbs tell us that every word of God proves true. Whatever He says goes.

Why is it good that God's promises always come true?

And the people of Israel journeyed from Rameses to Succoth, about
six hundred thousand men on foot, besides women and children.
Exodus 12:37

Each year in school, I would count down the days until summer break. I couldn't wait for it to get here. On summer break, my family would go to the beach and the mountains on vacation. I got to go camping with my church friends. I can't wait for summer.

In a much greater way, God's people couldn't wait for freedom. Then, the day finally came when God delivered them from Egypt. After the Passover, Pharaoh told God's people to leave. And they did. They went on an Exodus. That is what the Book of the Bible is named after. They had just begun their long journey. But at this point, no one knew where they were going. Not even Moses. But they had God leading them, and that's all they needed.

Why didn't God tell them where they were going?

"Consecrate to me all the firstborn. Whatever is the first to open the
womb among the people of Israel, both of man and of beast, is mine."
Exodus 13:1

God and Pharaoh were very different kings. They are about as opposite as day and night. God is good and righteous. Pharaoh was evil. Pharaoh was willing to kill all the children out of fear. But God wanted the children to live. When God asks the people to consecrate their firstborn children to him, He asks them to promise that they will live for him.

God had special jobs that he needed to do. Some of the jobs were about building a place of worship, and other jobs were about helping people worship God. So, Israelites promised to give their firstborn to Him so that they could have these special jobs. They were showing Him that they trusted Him.

What kind of special jobs does God give us today?

*And the Lord went before them by day in a pillar of cloud to lead
them along the way, and by night in a pillar of fire to give them
light, that they might travel by day and by night.*
Exodus 13:21

Have you ever played the game "Follow the Leader?" It's a fun game where you follow a leader in a single file line. Whatever that leader does, all the followers have to do. If he jumps over a crack in the sidewalk, the whole line has to jump through that same crack. If he walks backwards with his tongue sticking out, so does the rest of the line.

Now that God's people were getting out of Egypt, they had a leader to follow. Although you might expect Moses, God said that He would be the leader. He would lead them by cloud during the day and fire at night.

What makes a good leader?

*When the king of Egypt was told that the people had fled, the
mind of Pharaoh and his servants was changed toward the
people, and they said, "What is this we have done, that we have
let Israel go from serving us?"*
Exodus 14:5

It's hard to imagine that Pharaoh would try again, but he did. God's people have already made their way out of Egypt. God has already sent 10 plagues to convince Pharaoh to let them go. Pharaoh's son died because of all this. You would think that he would just let God's people go.

But he takes one last chance at it. He sends his armies to chase after God's people. This choice will cost him dearly. Pharaoh is going to have to learn the hard way that you cannot win a fight against the God of Israel.

Have you ever learned a lesson the hard way?

When Pharaoh drew near, the people of Israel lifted up their eyes,
and behold, the Egyptians were marching after them, and they
feared greatly. And the people of Israel cried out to the Lord.
Exodus 14:10

I'm getting older. One of the things that comes with getting older is getting forgetful. I used to be able to remember things. Now, I have to write down everything I need to do on an application on my phone. It can be frustrating walking into a room only to forget why I got up to go there in the first place.

Pharaoh forgot how powerful God was, so he chased after His people. And now God's people have forgotten how powerful God is. They are fearful of Pharaoh and his army. This is amazing to me because God stands before them as a pillar of cloud and fire. And still, they fear Pharaoh more.

Why do we forget how powerful God is sometimes?

The Lord will fight for you, and you have only to be silent.
Exodus 14:14

When I was in high school, I played football on the football team. I'm pretty small, so I didn't win many battles on the field. One day during practice, we did this drill where two people had to fight over a towel. I was put up against one of the biggest and strongest people. I knew there was no way I could win, but I tried my hardest.

He swung me around like a doll. Within seconds, he had torn the towel out of my hands. To my surprise, he came up to me afterward and said he was impressed that I fought so hard. He said if anyone picked on me, I should let him know. He would defend me. In a greater way, God promises to defend His people in every battle.

Have you ever had someone defend you?

*Lift up your staff, and stretch out your hand over the sea and divide
it, that the people of Israel may go through the sea on dry ground.*
Exodus 14:16

Following God takes faith. This means that you have to trust Him even when you don't know His plan. God's people had been chased to the edge of a sea. Behind them was an army they could not win a fight against. In front of them was a sea they could not swim across. They were stuck.

God told Moses to put his staff in the water. What good would that do? But Moses, in faith, stuck his staff in the water, and something amazing happened. The sea split in two and left a dry path for God's people to cross.

What is faith?

*The waters returned and covered the chariots and the horsemen;
of all the host of Pharaoh that had followed them into the sea, not
one of them remained.*
Exodus 14:28

After God's people crossed the sea, Pharaoh's army tried to follow them. But God would not allow His people to be taken back. Once Pharaoh's army was in the middle of the path, God sent the waters of the sea crashing back down on them. In one instant, the entire army was washed away.

God's people were saved. God kept His promise. All they had to do was trust Him, and He would provide for all of their needs. He would defend them in the battle. He would be their God, and they would be His people.

What do you think that would have looked like?

*Israel saw the great power that the Lord used against the
Egyptians, so the people feared the Lord, and they believed in the
Lord and in his servant Moses.*
Exodus 14:31

I'm scared of heights. I have always joked that God made me short for a reason. I don't like climbing too high. Fear can be a good thing. It keeps us safe. It helps us to realize when there is danger. So what does the Bible mean when it says that God's people feared God? Were they scared of Him like I am of heights?

I think that's part of it, but not the whole thing. In this verse, it says two things. They feared God, and they believed in the Lord. Fearing God is not just being scared of Him. It's realizing just how big He is and how small we are. It's accepting that we need Him.

Why do you think we need to fear God?

*I will sing to the Lord, for he has triumphed gloriously;
the horse and his rider he has thrown into the sea.*
Exodus 15:1

Christians are people who sing. The Bible has a whole book in it that is nothing but songs. It's called the Book of Psalms. Throughout the Bible, you can read different songs that God's people sang to Him and about Him. After they crossed the Red Sea, God's people stopped on the other side and sang His praises.

When was the last time you sang a song to God? It's a wonderful thing to do. It shows Him how much you love Him. And it can help you remember all the things that He has done for you. We all learn lyrics to songs. Why not take the time to learn the lyrics to a song about Jesus?

What is your favorite Christian song?

You have led in your steadfast love the people whom you have redeemed; you have guided them by your strength to your holy abode.
Exodus 15:13

I am training to run 10k in a few months. If you don't know, a 10k is a race that is a little over 6 miles long. I am expecting to run for over an hour before I complete the race. That's a long time to run and a long distance to travel. The only way I will be able to accomplish my goal is by training every day and not stopping. I have to be steadfast in my run.

God's love for His people is steadfast. He keeps running after us even when we make mistakes and run away from Him. Take Israel, for example. They were on the run from Egypt, and God was with them every step of the way.

What does it mean for God's love to be steadfast?

You will bring them in and plant them on your own mountain, the place, O Lord, which you have made for your abode, the sanctuary, O Lord, which your hands have established.
Exodus 15:17

Do you have a garden? My grandma did for most of my childhood. We only visited her a few times a year, but we did the same thing every time. We would walk down to her garden and help pick green beans and tomatoes. A fresh tomato from the garden is so tasty.

God says that He plants His people where He wants them. The Promised Land they are headed to is a place where they can grow. It's a home they can grow up in. It's a land where they can stay for a long, long time. It's a place where God will cultivate them like they are a garden.

How does God grow His people?

And the people grumbled against Moses, saying, "What shall we drink?"
Exodus 15:24

On every road trip that I have ever been on, there comes a moment when people start to grumble. Either they get hungry, or they get thirsty. Maybe they need to use the restroom. Or maybe they are just sick and tired of being stuck in a vehicle all day long. Have you ever felt like grumbling? Grumbling is something that God's people become known for while they are in the wilderness.

The grumbling is particularly painful to hear in light of the great salvation. They have experience. Think about it. God just saved them from a massive army and led them across a great sea on dry land. If he can do all of that, then what would stop him from providing for them? And yet, what do they do when they get to the other side of the sea? They grumble. It is easy for us to forget what God is capable of doing for us.

Why do people grumble to God?

DAY 52: PROVISION

Then they came to Elim, where there were twelve springs of water
and seventy palm trees, and they encamped there by the water.
Exodus 15:27

It is a good thing that I am not God. It is probably a good thing that you are not God, either. Because if I were God, then I would have been furious with Israel when they grumbled in the desert. I would have taken my anger out on them and let them get to the point of near death first before alleviating anything. How could they be so ungrateful?

But what does God do? He provides for them. Even when they are not thankful. And even when they forget his kindness so quickly. God provides for them all the water they could ever need in a safe oasis away from the enemy. That is grace.

How is God gracious to His people?

*and the people of Israel said to them, "Would that we had died by
the hand of the Lord in the land of Egypt, when we sat by the
meat pots and ate bread to the full, for you have brought us out
into this wilderness to kill this whole assembly with hunger."*
Exodus 16:3

If you thought the grumbling was bad last time, just wait. Instead of being thirsty, God's people complain about being hungry. The complaint is understanding, but what is not OK is the question of whether or not God loves them. They said that they would rather go back to slavery in Egypt than stay out in the wilderness.

They are questioning whether God even cares to provide for them. This can be frustrating to read because we know that just a few verses ago, God had already provided for them. But it is a good reminder for us just how quickly we can forget how kind our God is when life gets hard and people are mean. We can forget about God altogether.

Why do people forget about God?

*Then the Lord said to Moses, "Behold, I am about to rain bread from heaven for
you, and the people shall go out and gather a day's portion every day, that I may test
them, whether they will walk in my law or not.*
Exodus 16:4

God graciously provides for his people again. He promises to rain down bread from heaven to feed them. But this time there is something added to the provision. He said that He is going to do this in a way that tests God's people.

The test is simply this. The bread that will come from heaven will only last for one day. If they gather more than they can eat, it will just rot away. And if they do not gather on the weekend, then they will not have any for their day of worship and rest. This test is to see whether they will trust him to provide every single day.

How does God provide for you every day?

On the seventh day some of the people went out to gather, but they found none.
Exodus 16:27

God is gracious and kind to his people. He will lavish his love on them and give them everything that they need. But he will not do it without any kind of rules or regulations. He wants to know that they love him in return. He wants to know that they trust him.

Sadly, some of God's people did not trust him. When they went out on the seventh day, they found no food for them. And this is exactly what God said would happen if they did not gather enough on the sixth day. If we fail to trust God, we should not be surprised when he does not provide for us.

Why is it hard to trust God?

DAY 56: TASTE AND SEE

Now the house of Israel called its name manna. It was like coriander seed, white, and the taste of it was like wafers made with honey.
Exodus 16:31

There is a verse in the Bible that I have come to love. It says that we should taste and see that the Lord is good. The bread that God provided for his people tasted like bread with honey on it. It was sweet and good to eat. One of my favorite foods is buttermilk biscuits with honey on them.

So, I can imagine just how wonderful it was to taste the bread that God provided.

Taste and see the Lord is good is not usually about what goes into your mouth, but what goes into your heart. When you trust God and see how faithful he can be, it tastes sweet to your soul, like honey on your lips.

How can you taste and see that God is good?

35

But the people thirsted there for water, and the people grumbled against Moses and said, "Why did you bring us up out of Egypt, to kill us and our children and our livestock with thirst?"
Exodus 17:3

Have you ever played the blame game with someone? When I was in middle school, I got into an argument with one of my friends. He said that I threw my shoe at him during band class. I was adamant that I did not. And so we blamed each other and our friends back and forth until everybody was upset.

Moses and God's people are in the midst of a blaming match. They are grumbling again about being thirsty, and they are now blaming Moses for leading them into the wilderness. The man who led them out of slavery is their enemy. When we are tempted to blame other people for the challenges we face in life, we can lose sight of what is true. The next time you want to blame somebody else, take a moment and pray to see what is going on.

Why do we blame others for our problems?

Behold, I will stand before you there on the rock at Horeb, and you shall strike the rock, and water shall come out of it, and the people will drink." And Moses did so in the sight of the elders of Israel.
Exodus 17:6

This is one of my favorite stories in the Bible because it reminds me of Jesus. It doesn't seem like it at first, but I promise you it tells you about Jesus. The people were in desperate need of water. If they did not get water, they would die. And so God told Moses to strike a rock with the staff and break it. And from that rock, they would find water to save their lives.

We need saving, too. We need the living water. We need grace from God to save our souls. And Jesus was the rock that had to be broken to save us. He was struck by the staff of the Cross, and by his blood, we can be saved.

How is Jesus like the rock?

But Moses' hands grew weary, so they took a stone and put it under him, and he sat on it, while Aaron and Hur held up his hands, one on one side, and the other on the other side. So his hands were steady until the going down of the sun.
Exodus 17:12

We all need help sometimes. We might need help with our homework or help to figure out what to do. And it is wonderful to have a friend when you need help. Moses had some excellent friends.

Israel got into a war with another nation, and God would allow Israel to win the battle as long as Moses held his staff in the air. But the battle lasted for hours and days. And so Moses, his hands and arms got tired. So, when the staff was lowered, Israel began to lose. Moses and his friends came and made a seat for him. And they held his arms up for him. What a wonderful thing it is to have friends.

How can you be a friend today?

You and the people with you will certainly wear yourselves out, for the thing is too heavy for you. You are not able to do it alone.
Exodus 18:18

Your parents have a lot of jobs. They have a lot of responsibilities. Sometimes, they have to be the ones who earn money. Sometimes, they have to be your doctor. Sometimes, they have to be the ones who feed and clean you. They have a lot of jobs.

Moses had a lot of jobs, too. He was the leader of God's people. But he was also the judge for them. If they ever had any issues, they would come to him to solve them. Moses's father-in-law, Jethro, saw that Moses was getting too tired of doing all of these jobs. He gave some good advice that we can learn from, too. He told him to not do more than he could handle. And he told him to let his friends help out. If you feel overwhelmed, you can reach out to your friends and your family to get help like Moses did.

Who can help you if you need help?

*So Moses listened to the voice of his father-in-law and did all
that he had said.*
Exodus 18:24

There are two parts to getting advice. Part number one is that you have to admit that you need help and ask for it. Part number two is following the advice that you get. It does no good to ask how to make a sandwich but then never actually go and make the sandwich, so if Moses hadn't listened to Jethro, his life wouldn't have gotten any better.

But Moses did listen to the advice of his father-in-law. And the advice that he gave worked. His life got better, and his job got easier. When we listen to our parents and get advice from our friends, our lives can get better, too. God can speak to us through our friends and family to help us figure out how to do things and solve problems.

When have you asked for advice?

*Now therefore, if you will indeed obey my voice and keep my
covenant, you shall be my treasured possession among all peoples,
for all the earth is mine;*
Exodus 19:5

I think the Pirates are cool. I used to like to read stories about them and watch movies about them. How much fun would it be to sell out in the ocean and to find hidden treasure? Pirates look for treasure because of how valuable it is. Gold, rubies, and all kinds of jewels can be found hidden in the ground in these boxes. What better job could there be?

Did you know that God calls us hidden treasure? His people are like precious gold and jewels in his eyes. He loves them, he searches for them, and when he finds his people, he keeps them forever. If you are a Christian, you are a treasure to God. And he will keep you forever.

Why does God treasure his people?

*Then Moses brought the people out of the camp to meet God, and
they took their stand at the foot of the mountain.*
Exodus 19:17

Have you ever thought about what it would be like to meet God? It won't be like what is shown on TV and in books sometimes. God is not an old man with a long white beard sitting on a golden throne. God is spirit. So what will it be like to meet him? I don't know that for sure, but I do know what it was like when Moses met God.

God appeared to Moses in a thick cloud that sometimes looked like it was on fire. He entered into the glory of God, and it was like a bright light. Can you imagine what that would have been like? I would think he was scared at some point. And he was probably in all those other points. When Moses went to the mountain, he met with God and learned exactly how God wanted his people to live.

What do you think it will be like to meet God?

*And the Lord said to Moses, "Go down and warn the people, lest
they break through to the Lord to look and many of them perish."*
Exodus 19:21

God is holy. This means that God is perfect. He is perfectly good and perfectly kind. He is perfectly just and perfectly right. This is a great thing for him and a scary thing for us. Because we are not perfect. We are not holy. And God cannot be with imperfect people.

The punishment for sin is death because God cannot be with sinful people. This is why Jesus is so important to us. He died on the cross so that we would not have to. He took our punishment for sin. And because of what he did, we can enter into the presence of God. How amazing is that!

What does it mean for God to be holy?

"You shall have no other gods before me.
Exodus 20:3

When Moses went to the mountain to meet with God, God gave him a bunch of rules. These were rules that told Moses how life worked best. But you can summarize all the rules into 10 Commandments. The first of those 10 Commandments is that you should have no other gods before the god of Israel.

This is the only way that life with God works. If there is another God that you follow, then you cannot love the God of the Bible. To put anyone else before him would be to sin against the holy God. If you believe in Jesus, then he will be the only God that you can trust forever.

Do you know anyone who trusts another god?

You shall not make for yourself a carved image, or any likeness of
anything that is in heaven above, or that is in the earth beneath,
or that is in the water under the earth.
Exodus 20:4

The second Commandment can be hard for us to understand. Not many of us have idols in our house. We don't keep little statues of different gods around. And we don't make them either. But this was a really common thing in the time of the Bible. And so God included this in the 10 Commandments.

Even though we don't have little statues of gods in our homes, we do have little idols all around us. Our phones can become more important to us than other people. Our money can make us feel more powerful than others. What we wear and who we hang out with can be the most important thing for us at times. And when that happens, those things become little idols in our lives.

What in your life might become an idol?

You shall not take the name of the Lord your God in vain, for the
Lord will not hold him guiltless who takes his name in vain.
Exodus 20:7

If you ever get the chance to meet the president of the United States, what will you call him or her? I doubt that you would call them buddy or Friend. And you definitely wouldn't call them a bad name. You would call them something respectful. Maybe you would say good morning, Mr. President. Or it would be nice to meet you, Madame President. You would give their name the honor that it is due.

This is what the third commandment is all about. It is not disrespectful to use God's name. Some people will use God's name instead of cussing. But that is disrespectful. It is taking his name in vain. We need to be careful about how we talk to him and how we talk about him to other people.

How can we honor God's name?

Remember the Sabbath day, to keep it holy.
Exodus 20:8

Going to church every week is a really important thing for a Christian. It is so important that God made it number four on his rules list. Now, that is not exactly what it says, but that is what it means. The Sabbath day was a day for rest and worship. In the beginning, that day was Saturday. And because Jesus rose from the grave on Sunday, God's people rested and worshiped on Sunday.

God wants us to protect one day a week to worship him with other Christians. This is what he means when he says to keep it holy. That means to keep it separate from every other day of the week. It's supposed to be special. This means that we should do everything we can to go to church, even if it means that we miss someone's birthday party or a ball game.

Where do you go to church?

*Honor your father and your mother, that your days may be long in
the land that the Lord your God is giving you.*
Exodus 20:12

Do you have a good mom and dad? I mean, do you have a mom and dad who love you, take care of you, and want the best for you? Most kids in the world have that. Some kids sadly don't. But if you do, this commandment should be easy for you. You should love to honor your father and mother because they love you.

But sometimes, we don't honor our parents. Sometimes, we don't listen to them, or we don't obey them right away. Sometimes, we get frustrated and say mean things to them under our breath. Be careful. They love you so much, and they want the best for you. And the best thing for you to do in return is to honor them.

How can you honor your father and mother?

You shall not murder.
Exodus 20:13

Odds are you have not murdered anyone. Let's be honest. There are not many kids in the world who have ended an innocent person's life. And so this command seems easy to follow, too. But it gets much harder when we think about what Jesus said.

In the book of Matthew, Jesus tells us that if we keep anger and hatred in our hearts, it's like killing somebody. In other places in the Bible, we are told that our words can kill people, too. We can say something about someone that hurts them so badly it can feel like they are dying. So, let's be careful with the kind of feelings we keep in our hearts and the kind of words that come out of our mouths.

How can our words hurt others?

You shall not commit adultery.
Exodus 20:14

If you don't have one already, one day, you will have a girlfriend. She will be someone that you love and want to care for. Hopefully, every relationship you have will end happily. But sometimes, it can be very sad and painful. This is why God says that you shall not commit adultery. In other words, God is telling all of his people to be faithful in each of their relationships.

If you have a girlfriend, they do not flirt with other girls. If you get married one day, then do not act like you are married to another person. We are called to be faithful and kind to the people that we are in a relationship with. We need to be good friends, boyfriends, and husbands.

How is God a good friend to us?

You shall not steal.
Exodus 20:15

I like superhero movies. It is fun to watch the superhero catch the bad guy. Some of the coolest scenes in those movies are when the bad guy is trying to rob a bank. They have to use all kinds of tools and equipment to try to crack the safe that holds all of the money. And the superhero comes in and stops them just before they get away with all of the money bags.

When we think of the command not to steal, this is the kind of thing that we think about. Big items that are stolen or what come into our mind. But the reality is that if we take anything that is not ours, it is stealing. If we take someone's pencil without asking, or we grab an extra piece of candy that doesn't belong to us, that is stealing too. It shows that our hearts are capable of stealing small things and eventually big things if we don't turn to God.

Why do people steal things?

You shall not bear false witness against your neighbor.
Exodus 20:16

I go to the corn maze every year. They are so much fun. You get to try to figure out your way through this crazy maze in the middle of a cornfield. The key to success in getting out is to remember where you've been. Otherwise, you'll get lost and keep going around in circles. God tells us not to bear false witness against our neighbor. This is a fancy way of saying don't lie.

One of the really difficult things about lying is you have to keep telling other lies to cover up the original lie. It's like walking around in a maze. You always have to remember what you said last time before you tell a new lie. Eventually, you get lost and trapped inside of it. For your good, God says do not lie to other people. It is the truth that sets us free. The truth helps us to get out of the maze.

Have you ever been caught in a lie?

You shall not covet your neighbor's house; you shall not covet your neighbor's wife, or his male servant, or his female servant, or his ox, or his donkey, or anything that is your neighbor's.
Exodus 20:17

When I grew up, I was jealous of my neighbor. My neighbor had a cool trampoline. We didn't have one at our house. And we didn't get to go to our neighbor's house very often because it was across the street on a very busy road. I would sit on my front porch and look across the road and see my neighbor jumping around and having a wonderful time.

That is called coveting. The funny thing about coveting is that it gets you nowhere. You can spend all day long coveting what someone else has and making yourself feel miserable. But what does that accomplish? Does that help you at all? No. Coveting just does damage to your own heart. We ought to be thankful for all that we have, even if it is not very much. Thankfulness does well to our hearts.

What are you thankful for today?

Moses said to the people, "Do not fear, for God has come to test you, that the fear of him may be before you, that you may not sin."
Exodus 20:20

God takes sin seriously. He wants all of his people to follow him closely. And so, in his kindness, he gave us all of the rules that we needed to follow. And he even summarizes all of the rules into just 10 main rules. He gives us all these things so that we will not sin. Because if we sin, we earn the penalty of death.

In God's grace, he only gives us the law, but he gives us a way to find forgiveness. Even if we sin, he shows us the way forward. He sent his son Jesus to take the punishment for our sins on the cross. If we place our faith in him, then we can live lives that honor God at all times.

How does the Law keep us from sin?

DAY 76: TRAVELERS

You shall not wrong a sojourner or oppress him, for you were sojourners in the land of Egypt.
Exodus 22:21

God loves all people. But he seems to have a special kind of love for people who are in trouble. In this verse, we see that he has a special love for those who are traveling. This doesn't mean those who are on a road trip but those who have to move their lives all together. There may be a war that they had to leave or a hardship they are fleeing from.

God makes sure that his people will welcome the traveler. He wants to make sure that anyone who is oppressed can find refuge and rest with Christians. So if you ever have anyone new in your class at school, be the place of refuge and rest for them. Welcome to Traveler.

How can you welcome the traveler this week?

You shall not mistreat any widow or fatherless child.
Exodus 22:22

I have had the distinct privilege of adopting my son. He was born in a foreign country to another woman. But he is my son. We treat him no differently than any of our other children. There's a love that exists for my son that is unique. This is the kind of love that God has for widows and orphans.

Typically, widows and orphans are in danger of not being taken care of. But God loves everyone and wants to take care of everyone. The primary way that he takes care of people is through the local church. He uses his people to love others. We should mirror the heart of God and try to take care of those who cannot take care of themselves.

What does your church do to love orphans and widows?

Behold, I send an angel before you to guard you on the way and to
bring you to the place that I have prepared.
Exodus 23:20

God is leading his people on a long journey. It began in Egypt while they were slaves. He led them across the Red Sea and into the wilderness. But their journey is not over. Neither are the battles that they have to fight. And so God promises to lead them by an angel into the place that he has prepared for them.

The promised land that they are headed toward is occupied by other people. Israel will have to fight and claw their way into the promised land. But God will not make them do it alone. He will pave the way for them so that he can keep his promise to them forever. Whatever challenges you face, please know that the God of angel armies goes with you.

What challenges are you facing?

*Moses came and told the people all the words of the Lord and all
the rules. And all the people answered with one voice and said,
"All the words that the Lord has spoken we will do."*
Exodus 24:3

Have you ever been to a wedding? There is a famous moment towards the end of the wedding where the pastor asks both the bride and the groom if they will take the other person to be their husband or wife. That is when the bride and the groom both say, I do. At that moment, they promised to win another and that they would stay together until death do them part.

When Moses comes down the mountain with the law of God in hand, he asks them if they will commit themselves to God. And they altogether say we do. They promise to love and follow him for the rest of their lives. All that he has spoken they will do. Will you?

Will you follow God forever?

*And Moses wrote down all the words of the Lord. He rose early
in the morning and built an altar at the foot of the mountain,
and twelve pillars, according to the twelve tribes of Israel.*
Exodus 24:4

as you get older, you will find out that a lot of people like to give you written documents. Grocery stores give you physical receipts. Anytime you make a deal with somebody, there is often a paper trail to follow. We do this because we are prone to forget what we agreed on, and sometimes, we need proof of what was said.

When Moses came down off the mountain with the law, he had it written down. He wanted proof of what God said to him. And God did not want us to forget what he wanted us to do. And so he etched the words on stone tablets so that his people could have them forever. What a gift it is to have the word of God written down.

Why did God write down His Law?

*And they saw the God of Israel. There was under his feet as it were a
pavement of sapphire stone, like the very heaven for clearness.*
Exodus 24:10

So far in the book of Exodus, God has been pictured like a pillar of cloud
and a pillar of fire. He has shown himself to Moses as a fire in a burning
bush. But this picture of God seems different. He is described as someone who
stands on precious stones. This can be hard for us to imagine.

But this is the same picture of God that we see in the Book of Revelation.
He is someone so mighty that the most precious of stones are easy for him to
walk on. If we see money on the ground, we would pick it up. But God is so
mighty and so powerful that he does not need money or precious stones.

How does this verse change your view of God?

*Moses entered the cloud and went up on the mountain. And
Moses was on the mountain forty days and forty nights.*
Exodus 24:18

Think about that verse for just a minute. 40 days and 40 nights is a long
time. That is over a month. For 40 days and 40 nights, Moses was on top of the
mountain. But even more importantly, he was in the presence of God. He was
living with God for over a month.

I don't know if you have ever experienced feeling close to God. But in this
moment, Moses couldn't have been closer. For 40 days, he got to sit in the presence of God, talk with him, and hear from him. As a Christian, you don't have
to wait until you have a mountaintop experience to be close to God. The Bible
promises that the Holy Spirit lives within each of us who have placed our faith
in Jesus. We can be close to him right now as we pray.

How can we be close to God?

Speak to the people of Israel, that they take for me a contribution. From every man whose heart moves him you shall receive the contribution for me.
Exodus 25:2

If you have ever saved up money to buy a new toy, then you know what this verse is all about. They are trying to raise money to build a sanctuary for God. So God tells Moses to ask everyone in Israel to give whatever they can. Whatever they feel led to give by God, they should.

Some people could only give a few dollars, while others could provide whole portions of the sanctuary by themselves. The important part about this first is to see that all of God's people needed to be all in. Everyone needed to do what they could, even if it was just a little bit.

What can you contribute to God?

They shall make an ark of acacia wood. Two cubits and a half shall be its length, a cubit and a half its breadth, and a cubit and a half its height.
Exodus 25:10

When people think about the Ark, they think about Noah and the giant boat that he built that survived the flood. But The Ark, which is talked about in this reverse, is very different. It is a relatively small wooden box that is covered in gold. Inside the Ark, Moses put the 10 Commandments and his staff.

This was meant to be a reminder that God was like Noah's ark for them. He carried them through safety. As long as he was present with them, he would protect them from the dangerous waters of life.

Do you have anything that reminds you of God's presence?

There I will meet with you, and from above the mercy seat,
from between the two cherubim that are on the ark of the
testimony, I will speak with you about all that I will give you in
commandment for the people of Israel.
Exodus 25:22

On top of the ark of the covenant was something called the mercy seat. This was probably the most precious place in all of Israel. It was on the mercy seat that God would sit and listen to his people. Incredibly, God would sit and forgive his people on the mercy seat. That is how it got its name.

Mercy is when we do not get what we deserve. We all deserve punishment because we all failed God. But we do not get punishment. Instead, we get mercy. Every time we go to God in prayer we can know for sure that he will be merciful to us today.

Why do we need mercy?

You shall put the mercy seat on the ark of the testimony in the
Most Holy Place.
Exodus 26:34

I am not a fan of hard-boiled eggs, but my kids love them. What is cool about hard-boiled eggs is that they have three distinct layers. There is the shell, the egg, the white, and the yolk. When it is boiled, you can see all the layers clearly when you cut it in half. The most holy place is like the egg yolk.

God had his people build a mobile sanctuary. Inside of the mobile sanctuary was the most holy place. And inside of the most holy place was the ark of the covenant of God. It was called the most holy place because that is where the holy God would meet with them. Only once a year could a priest enter into the most holy place.

Do you know of a place that seems holy to you?

So Aaron shall bear the names of the sons of Israel in the breastpiece of judgment on his heart, when he goes into the Holy Place, to bring them to regular remembrance before the Lord.
Exodus 28:29

Every year, the priest would enter into the most holy place and ask God to forgive his people. Each year, the priest would wear a coat with all of the names of the tribes of Israel on it. The reason he wore this is because he was representing everybody in Israel. He took all of their names before God and asked for forgiveness.

Can you imagine having that kind of responsibility? In a greater way, this is exactly what Jesus did for us on the cross. Although he was practically naked on the cross, he stood in our place. He asked for the forgiveness of all of our sins. And there, God showed him wrath while showing us mercy.

Why did the priests wear the names of the sons of Israel?

I will dwell among the people of Israel and will be their God.
Exodus 29:45

We all have people that we love to be around. It may be our best friend from school or our brother or sister. A lot of people just simply love to be with their mom. God loves to be with us. He loves to dwell among his people. That is what he has been doing from the very beginning of the Bible.

In the Garden of Eden, at the beginning, God walked with his people. And even after we broke our relationship with him by sin, he has made different ways to be with us. Jesus is the wonderful way that God is with us now. He walked among us and died for us. And now his spirit lives within us.

Why does God want to dwell among us?

And I have filled him with the Spirit of God, with ability and intelligence, with knowledge and all craftsmanship.
Exodus 31:3

God gives us everything that we need. When he told Israel to build a sanctuary for him, he told them to gather all of the materials they would need. He had everybody contribute something. Once all of the materials were gathered, he then asked everybody to pitch in and do something.

Behind all of that, do you realize that it was gone that provided everything everything? He is the one who gave them all the materials to begin with. And he is the one who gave them the ability to build and craft things. There is no possible way they would've ever built the sanctuary. Had it not been for God giving them all that they need.

What kind of abilities has God given you?

And he gave to Moses, when he had finished speaking with him on Mount Sinai, the two tablets of the testimony, tablets of stone, written with the finger of God.
Exodus 31:18

The word of God came from the hand of God. We can trust it. You can always trust the words of other people. Sometimes, they lie, and other times they forget. We can get facts confused or mixed up. But not God. He always tells us the truth. So, if his word comes from his hand, then it is 100% trustworthy.

This is wonderful news for us. If the Bible is from the hand of God, then we can have full confidence in it. We can know that exactly what he says is what he thinks. We never have to guess.

Why can we trust the Bible?

*And he received the gold from their hand and fashioned it with
a graving tool and made a golden calf. And they said, "These are
your gods, O Israel, who brought you up out of the land of Egypt!"*
Exodus 32:4

God's people got tired of waiting for Moses. He had gone back up the mountain to talk with God again, and they didn't know when he would come back. To be fair, he was gone for 40 days last time. They grew impatient and decided they needed to do something.

They went to Aaron, Moses' helper, and told him to make a golden calf. They wanted to worship the golden idol just like other nations. This was not good because God had just told them to make idols. They said they would obey, but they didn't. They were in for some trouble.

Have you ever done something you knew would get you in trouble?

*And the Lord said to Moses, "Go down, for your people, whom you
brought up out of the land of Egypt, have corrupted themselves.*
Exodus 32:7

Moses was completely unaware of what was going on back at camp. He had no idea that God's people had made the golden calf and started to worship it. Moses was enjoying his time with God and learning more about what it meant to follow Him. That was until God stopped what they were doing and told Moses to go back down the mountain.

How would you feel if your time with God got cut short because of someone else's mistake? I would be frustrated and sad. I would be ready to fight the people at the bottom of the mountain. Take time to make a prediction. What do you think Moses will do when he gets back?

When was a time when you got really mad?

*Now therefore let me alone, that my wrath may burn hot against them
and I may consume them, in order that I may make a great nation of you.*
Exodus 32:10

I do not know how mad you have been in the past. But God was so mad that He was ready to never speak to Israel again. He wanted to send another flood and start over again like He did with Noah and the Ark. Have you ever been that mad?

It's scary when someone is that upset with someone else. It's even scarier to think that God could be that mad at us. When we sin against Him, He does get mad. He's offended when we don't follow His rules because it shows Him that we think His way is not the best. If it wasn't for Jesus, we would be consumed by God's anger.

How does Jesus protect us from God's anger?

*But Moses implored the Lord his God and said, "O Lord, why does
your wrath burn hot against your people, whom you have brought out
of the land of Egypt with great power and with a mighty hand?"*
Exodus 32:11

I used to play tennis. It's such a fun sport. One way you play tennis is with a partner. That's called playing doubles tennis. What's fun about doubles tennis is that someone always has your back. If you miss a shot or cannot make it in time, your partner is there to help you out.

There are times in tennis when your partner steps in front of you and takes a shot that you're not ready for. When Moses "implored the Lord God" he was being a good partner. He stepped in front of Israel and turned God's anger away from them. In a greater way, Jesus did this for us when He died on the cross.

How can you turn away someone's anger?

*And as soon as he came near the camp and saw the calf and the
dancing, Moses' anger burned hot, and he threw the tablets out of
his hands and broke them at the foot of the mountain.*
Exodus 32:19

If you've ever played sports, then you've gotten mad playing that sport. When we get mad, we sometimes throw something in anger. Basketball players may slam the ball on the ground. Baseball players may toss their bat. Tennis players may hit their racket on the ground. Moses wasn't playing a game that day, but he threw something in his anger.

Moses threw the stone tablets with the Ten Commandments on them to the ground. They shattered. This was like a picture of what God's people had done. They had shattered the Law of God. What could help them now? How could they be saved?

How can we be saved from our sins?

*He took the calf that they had made and burned it with fire and
ground it to powder and scattered it on the water and made the
people of Israel drink it.*
Exodus 32:20

I don't know the right names for sports drinks. Some are called Berry Blast or Fruit Fusion. I just call them by their color. I like the blue and the orange sports drinks the best. The drink that Moses made for Israel that day was not a sports drink. It was a terrible punishment.

Moses ground the idol they made into a powder. He mixed it into the water. And he made God's people drink it. He wanted them to taste the bitterness of sin. He never wanted them to forget what worshipping idols will get you. Only by worshipping God alone can we taste the fresh living water He provides.

Why did Moses make them drink the idol?

And Aaron said, "Let not the anger of my lord burn hot.
You know the people, that they are set on evil."
Exodus 32:22

This verse teaches us a lot about us. When it says that God's people are "set on evil," it means that we are naturally sinful. We naturally do what we want to do. We naturally put ourselves first. We're bent towards sinning. This does not mean that we only do evil things all of the time. But it does mean that most of what we do is for us.

God wants to change this in us. He wants us to put Him first. He wants us to live our lives to love Him and love others. We need someone to change our nature. That person is Jesus. When we trust Him, He puts His Spirit in us. He helps us to live a new life.

When was a time that you put yourself first?

But now, if you will forgive their sin—but if not, please blot me
out of your book that you have written.
Exodus 32:32

When the Bible was written, they used ink, quills, and parchment. Most likely, you have never used those things. The quill is like a single bird's feather. The end of it is very similar to what our pens and pencils look like. They would dip the quill in a jar of black ink and write with it on a scroll made of parchment.

If they ever made a mistake, they had no eraser to use. You can't just wipe up ink off of paper. If they wanted to erase something, they had to blot it out. They would dab ink over the word. They would cover it completely. All those who place their faith in Jesus have their sin blotted out.

What does it mean for our sin to be blotted out?

*Then the Lord sent a plague on the people, because they made the
calf, the one that Aaron made.*
Exodus 32:25

God had forgiven them of their sin. The idol was made. It was destroyed. God was willing to forgive their sin. But this didn't mean that there was no punishment left. Like when you don't obey your parents, they love and forgive you every time. But there is usually still a punishment you have to go through.

This punishment for Israel was a plague. You should remember that from Egypt. That's what God sent to the Egyptians to tell them to let His people go. God is telling His people, if you don't follow my law, you'll be treated like those who don't follow my law.

How is life following God better than life not following Him?

*"Go up to a land flowing with milk and honey; but I will not go up among
you, lest I consume you on the way, for you are a stiff-necked people."*
Exodus 33:3

At the very beginning of this book, I told you that God's people were on a long journey home. God had made a promise to Abraham that He would make him into a nation and that His people would live in a Promised Land. God reminds His people of this place, their home.

God tells them that it will be a land flowing with milk and honey. This means that it will have everything they need. It will have cattle for milk and meat. It will have plants, flowers, bees, and honey. It will be like a beautiful garden paradise. No matter how "stiff-necked" we can be at times, God promises to take us home.

What do you think the Promised Land looked like?

*Thus the Lord used to speak to Moses face to face, as a man speaks
to his friend. When Moses turned again into the camp, his assistant
Joshua the son of Nun, a young man, would not depart from the tent.*
Exodus 33:11

Who is your best friend? I had a best friend named Kinden while I was growing up. We had so much fun together. Back then, we didn't have cell phones or instant messaging. The only time I got to talk to him was if we were together in person. I had to be face-to-face with him to hear from him.

God and Moses spoke to each other like friends. The Bible says they spoke face to face. What an incredible thing to think about. We don't get to speak to God face to face. But we do get to speak to Him heart to heart. Every prayer we pray goes directly from our hearts to His. No matter where you are, you can speak to Him.

When do you pray to God?

And he said, "My presence will go with you, and I will give you rest."
Exodus 33:14

Some nights, I have a hard time going to sleep. There are times when my mind won't stop thinking about what I have to do tomorrow. There are other times when I'm worried about something, and it's hard to fall asleep. Rest can be hard to get when you're anxious about something.

God gives us a promise in this verse. He says that His presence goes with us and that He will give us rest. When we know we are with God, we can have peace. This peace comes from knowing that He will always take care of us. If you're feeling anxious or worried, pray to God. Let His presence be your peace today.

Why does God's presence give us peace?

DAY 103: GOD'S GLORY

Moses said, "Please show me your glory."
Exodus 33:18

Moses loved God. He wanted to know everything about God. They were so close that Moses asked a dangerous question. He asked God to show Him His glory. In other words, He asked God not to hide anything from Him. He wanted to see all of God in all of His glory.

Our minds cannot comprehend the fullness of God. Our sinful hearts cannot stand before a perfect God. Moses was asking a dangerous thing with pure motivation. He wanted to give God all the honor he could, and that meant he wanted to see all of God. Let's ask this dangerous question.

When will you see the glory of God?

DAY 104: CLEFT OF THE ROCK

And while my glory passes by I will put you in a cleft of the rock,
and I will cover you with my hand until I have passed by.
Exodus 33:22

I love Old Testament verses that tell us about Jesus. We've seen a bunch of them already. Jesus told His disciples that the whole Bible is about Him. So, anytime we see something in the Bible that reminds us of Him, we should make note of it. Maybe highlight it in your Bible or write about it in the margin of the page.

The picture of Jesus we get in this verse is the cleft of the rock. God knew that if Moses saw Him in all of His glory, he would not live. So He hid Moses in the cleft, or the crack, of a rock. It's there that Moses was kept safe and was able to see some of God's glory. Jesus is our cleft in the rock. Because of Him, we can see the glory of God and be kept safe.

How is Jesus like the cleft of the rock?

*The Lord said to Moses, "Cut for yourself two tablets of stone like
the first, and I will write on the tablets the words that were on
the first tablets, which you broke.*
Exodus 34:1

In golf, there is something called a mulligan. That's like a do-over. If you hit a bad shot or make a mistake, you can try again. You can take a mulligan. Our God is a God of mulligans and do-overs. He gives second, third, and fourth chances.

God tells Moses that He is going to replace the stone tablets that Moses smashed on the ground in his anger earlier. God is going to give Moses and His people a second chance. This should give us a lot of comfort. No matter how much we mess up, God will always give us a mulligan.

When have you been given a second chance?

*The Lord passed before him and proclaimed, "The Lord, the Lord,
a God merciful and gracious, slow to anger, and abounding in
steadfast love and faithfulness,"*
Exodus 34:6

One of the great things about the Bible is that it tells us so much about God. If you want to know who he is and what he is like, all you have to do is read his word. Those first times, we are told that the Lord is merciful and gracious. It says that he is slow to anger and abounding and love and faithfulness.

This is the kind of God that I want to follow. This is the kind of God that I would trust my whole life with. It is no wonder that Israel was willing to leave everything behind to follow him in the wilderness. They trusted him because he was trustworthy.

What is your favorite thing about God?

*Keeping steadfast love for thousands, forgiving iniquity and
transgression and sin, but who will by no means clear the guilty,
visiting the iniquity of the fathers on the children and the
children's children, to the third and the fourth generation.*
Exodus 34:7

This verse can be confusing. It seems to say two things that are opposite of one another. At first, it says that God forgives sins. But then it says that he will buy by no means clear the guilty. How can he be a god of forgiveness and a God of punishment?

The answer to that question can only be found in Jesus. God forgives our sins because he put the guilt of our sins on Jesus. On the cross, Jesus took the whole punishment for our sins so that he could forgive us and, at the same time, not clear the guilty. On the cross, God was both Just and the justifier of his people.

How can God forgive and not forgive sins?

*You shall tear down their altars and break their pillars and cut
down their Asherim*
Exodus 34:13

Most of the time, we should try to avoid sin and bad situations. If we know that a certain video game makes us angry, then we should probably not play that video game. But you cannot always avoid sin. You cannot always hide from temptation. So, what do you do when you're faced with temptation?

God told Israel to fight their sin. Remember, one of the things that they struggled with was worshiping idols. So God said, "As you go along your journey, you should break the idols that you find." This was so that they would not be tempted to worship them. We need to do all the temptations and fight our sins.

How can you fight sin today?

When Moses came down from Mount Sinai, with the two tablets of the testimony in his hand as he came down from the mountain, Moses did not know that the skin of his face shone because he had been talking with God.
Exodus 34:29

Have you ever done something so exciting that you could not stop smiling afterwards? Sometimes, when we're looking forward to something amazing, it shows all over our faces. That is similar to what happened with Moses. He met with God and saw the glory of God. And when he came down off of the mountain, his face was shining with the glory of God.

There is a lesson for us to learn in this. When we spend time with God, it should be obvious to other people. We should be so amazed at what he says in the Bible that other people can see it on our faces.

How can we show others our excitement about God?

According to all that the Lord had commanded Moses, so the people of Israel had done all the work.
Exodus 39:42

God's people struggle to do what God says a lot of the time. But then there are wonderful moments in the Bible where they do exactly what they're supposed to do. This verse says that all that the Lord had commanded the people of Israel did. They were finally being obedient.

In our own lives, we have moments where we fail and do not obey God. But I hope that we have more moments where we do all that God says of us. Look back over the past day or the past and see how your life has been. Can you confidently say that you have done everything that the Lord has asked you to do?

How obedient have you been lately?

*Then the cloud covered the tent of meeting, and the glory of the
Lord filled the tabernacle.*
Exodus 40:34

If you are trying to study and understand the Bible, then you should make a note of this verse. It is verses like these that are important for God's people. There are times when the glory of God settles in a place and fills it. And there are times when the glory of God leaves.

When you reverse that says that the glory of God has filled a place, then you will know that God's people are as close to him as they have ever been. And there is no greater moment than when the glory of God dwells within Jesus. Through him, God himself walked among us. May we never experience the glory of God leaving us.

Why is the glory of God important?

*For the cloud of the Lord was on the tabernacle by day, and fire
was in it by night, in the sight of all the house of Israel throughout
all their journeys.*
Exodus 40:38

Our God is one of logic and order. He likes to work in the same ways as his people. If you remember, after God's people were taken out of Egypt, he led them by a pillar of cloud and a pillar of fire. Now, months later, he is doing the same thing again. They should know exactly how to follow him because they have done this before.

The same is true for us. God does not try to trick us. He doesn't change how he wants us to live or how to follow him. He tries to make it as simple and understandable as possible. You can expect God to work in similar ways throughout your life.

What is one way you know God works?

The Lord bless you and keep you
Numbers 6:24

Three verses in the Bible contain a very famous blessing. It is the blessing that is given to Erin. He is told to pronounce this blessing over cause people regularly. And God promises to bless his people in light of it. The first part is the Lord bless you and keep you.

To be blessed by God means to be provided for by him. And to be kept by God means to be protected from others by him. The only way God's people were going to make it to the promised land was if God both blessed and kept them. God promises to bless and keep us, too.

How has God blessed you?

The Lord make his face to shine upon you and be gracious to you
Numbers 6:25

What does the Bible mean when it says that we should want God's face to shine on us? How is that a blessing? Is it good, or is it scary? Let's think about it for a minute. If God's face is shining on us, that means that he is looking at us with love.

So when Aaron's blessing says that he wants the Lord's face to shine upon us. That means he wants God to always be looking out over us and caring about us. He explains that by saying that God will be gracious to you. This is kind of like when your mom or dad watches you play outside. They're looking out over you, and their hearts are filled with love.

What does it mean for God's face to shine upon us?

The Lord lift up his countenance upon you and give you peace.
Numbers 6:26

The older you get, the more you will appreciate this promise. The promise of peace is so incredibly precious. The older you get, the more responsibilities you will have. This means that you'll have a few more things to worry about and sometimes be stressed.

But God promises to give us his peace. As he lovingly looks out over us and keeps his eye on us. We can have peace. We know that he is in control, so there's nothing for us to worry about. This is why God is often called our father in the Bible. Because he cares for us like a parent cares for us.

How is God like a parent to us?

So shall they put my name upon the people of Israel, and I will bless them.
Numbers 6:27

Do you know what a pinky promise is? Maybe you don't do that. Growing up, if I wanted to show somebody that I was serious about the promise I was making, we would make a pinky promise. We would take our two pinkies and hold them together. That meant that I was as serious as I could be.

God is giving his people a pinky promise here. He has said over and over and over again that he will bless them. He is serious about this. They can count on him to be their God and bless them forever.

Why does God give so many promises?

*And if a stranger sojourns among you and would keep the
Passover to the Lord, according to the statute of the Passover and
according to its rule, so shall he do. You shall have one statute, both
for the sojourner and for the native.*
Numbers 9:14

If you have ever been to a new school or started a new sports team, then you know how scary it can be being a new person. And you also know how wonderful it can be to be invited in. To have someone invite you to sit down to lunch with them or to have someone show you how things work. That is a wonderful feeling.

A lot of the Bible is about Israel. But Israel has a job. They are to constantly invite people in. So when God says to let the traveler take the Passover with them, he is telling them to let them be part of his people. All are welcome in the people of God. This means that we should be welcoming to all people in our lives.

How can you be welcoming this week?

*At the command of the Lord the people of Israel set out, and at
the command of the Lord they camped. As long as the cloud rested
over the tabernacle, they remained in camp.*
Numbers 9:18

The more God's people trusted His promises, the more obedient they became. They saw that He would provide for them, protect them, love them, and keep them. Now, each time He moves, they move. They are becoming comfortable and continuing to obey God.

This is how the Christian life is supposed to be. We are supposed to trust the promises of God more and more. The more we trust Him, the more we will obey Him. The more we obey Him, the more He will prove that He is trustworthy. It's like a never-ending, wonderful cycle.

How do you need to obey God today?

*And the people of Israel set out by stages from the wilderness of
Sinai. And the cloud settled down in the wilderness of Paran.*
Numbers 10:12

This is a big moment for God's people. They have only traveled to a new location a few times. They went from Egypt to across the Red Sea. Then, they went from the Red Sea to Mount Sinai. They stayed at that mountain for a long time while God spoke to Moses.

Now they are on the road again. Not a paved road like we have today, but a dirt road through the wilderness. They were heading to a new place called Paran. Eventually, they would make it to the Promised Land. They had a long way to go, but they were off to a good start.

Do you think this would have been exciting or scary?

*And whenever the ark set out, Moses said, "Arise, O Lord, and let
your enemies be scattered, and let those who hate you flee before you."*
Numbers 10:35

There are all kinds of dogs in the world. I've got a dog with three legs. He runs fast, but he's pretty lazy most of the time. He prefers to lay in the sun all day. Some dogs like to go hunting. Hunters can train them to lie still until the right moment. At the right time, the hunter will tell them to arise and go get the prey.

Moses tells God to arise. Not like a dog under his command, but like a trusted friend or warrior. Moses knows that Israel cannot win the battles they will face. But He knows the promise of God, too. He knows that God will fight their battles for them. So he calls on the promise of God and says, "Arise, O Lord!"

What promise of God can you call on today?

*And the people complained in the hearing of the Lord about their
misfortunes, and when the Lord heard it, his anger was kindled,
and the fire of the Lord burned among them and consumed some
outlying parts of the camp.*
Numbers 11:1

There is a movie called Inside Out. In this movie, we get a glimpse into a girl's emotions. Each of them is described in different ways. The sadness emotion is blue and acts small. The happy emotion is yellow and bubbly. The anger emotion is red and spews flames of fire when he's upset.

This is the kind of picture we get of God's anger. Anger is not all that God is, but it is a part of Him. When He sees sin, it ignites a right anger in Him. Sometimes, He punishes people by sending fire to consume them. It's a scary thing to think about sometimes, but it's a good thing that God gets mad at the right things.

Why are fire and anger connected?

*But now our strength is dried up, and there is nothing at all but
this manna to look at.*
Numbers 11:6

Have you ever gone to the refrigerator or your pantry and said, "We have nothing to eat!"? Usually, when we say this, it's not entirely true. Usually, there is food in the refrigerator or pantry. But none of it looks appetizing to us. God's people are tired of eating manna. They are unsatisfied with it.

Although that can be frustrating, it is sinful. God provides our every need. When we reject his provision because it's not what we want, we are being selfish. The next time you're tempted to complain, even when you have all you need, be careful. You're complaining about God.

Why are we unsatisfied sometimes?

Moses said to the Lord, "Why have you dealt ill with your servant? And why have I not found favor in your sight, that you lay the burden of all this people on me?"
Numbers 11:11

One day, when you grow up, you'll end up leading something. You may be a coach for your kid's sports team. You may be a boss at a business. You may even grow up to be a pastor in a local church. However God uses you, you'll probably lead someone one day. Leadership comes with headaches.

People can be hard to lead. Some people don't want to listen to what you have to say. Some people will do the opposite of what you say just to make you mad. Just because leadership is hard doesn't mean we can throw in the towel. However, God uses us, and He expects us to stick it out in hard times.

Why should we stick it out in hard times?

I am not able to carry all this people alone; the burden is too heavy for me.
Numbers 11:14

When I carry groceries in from the van, I play a game. I try to see how many grocery bags I can carry at one time. My goal is to carry every bag on a grocery trip at one time. With a family of 5, that can be hard to do. What do you think happens if I grab too many bags? I either drop them or have to stop and let them down.

It's better for me to only grab what I can handle than to grab too much. Moses confesses to God that he feels like he has too much in his hands. He wants to drop the burden. God is kind to him. God offers to carry our burdens for us. We don't have to do anything alone.

Why does God offer to carry our burdens for us?

*And I will come down and talk with you there. And I will take
some of the Spirit that is on you and put it on them, and they
shall bear the burden of the people with you, so that you may not
bear it yourself alone.*
Numbers 11:17

Some things are too heavy for one person to carry. If you've ever moved houses, then you know this is true. Moving couches or tables from room to room is impossible to do alone. You need at least two people to share the load. This is true in moving furniture as much as it is true in life.

God has not designed us to live our lives alone. He wants us to rely on friends and family to help us in life. He has given them to us as a gift. He has equipped people in our lives in unique ways that can be there for us. Let's not forget the gift of family and friends. When you need help, ask.

What should you do if you need help with something?

*Then the Lord came down in the cloud and spoke to him, and
took some of the Spirit that was on him and put it on the seventy
elders. And as soon as the Spirit rested on them, they prophesied.
But they did not continue doing it.*
Numbers 11:25

Theology is a big fancy word. It means the study of God. Like math and reading in school, we need to study God too. We need to try to learn as much about Him as we can. In this verse, we learn something important about god. We learn that His Spirit empowers people.

In this verse, His Spirit empowers people to prophesy. In our lives, He empowers us in different ways. He empowers us to love people we don't like. He empowers us to forgive people who have hurt us. He empowers us to serve Him in His church. When you do something godly, it's because the Holy Spirit helped you do it.

How has God's Spirit empowered you?

Miriam and Aaron spoke against Moses because of the Cushite woman whom he had married, for he had married a Cushite woman.
Numbers 12:1

Moses broke a rule. God's people were to marry each other. They weren't supposed to marry people from other nations. The reason is that who you marry will influence you. If you marry a baker, you'll learn about baking. If you marry a painter, you'll learn about art. If you marry someone who doesn't love God, you'll learn not to love God.

Because Moses broke this rule, Miriam and Aaron confronted him about it. They were family, Moses' siblings. We need people that will call us out when we make mistakes. We call this being held accountable. You're a good person when you gently and lovingly hold others accountable for their actions.

Does anyone hold you accountable?

And Moses cried to the Lord, "O God, please heal her—please."
Numbers 12:13

Prayer is a wonderful thing. It's a way for us to talk to the God who created everything. Not only did He create everything, He is in charge of everything. There isn't anything that happens that He isn't aware of. This is why some of our prayers should be prayers for healing.

If you have a friend or family member who is sick or hurt, you should pray for them. Go to God with your concern. He can heal them. He can help. He may decide not to. But we shouldn't expect Him to heal anyone if we don't ask for it. He even said, "Ask, and you shall receive."

Who can you pray for today?

*Send men to spy out the land of Canaan, which I am giving to
the people of Israel. From each tribe of their fathers you shall send
a man, every one a chief among them.*
Numbers 13:2

On this long journey home, God's people made it to the front door of the Promised Land. It is not a real front door. It's not a house. It's a big piece of land. There are cities and whole nations who live there right now. This is why God's people decide to send spies into the land.

The spies' job is to take a look around without being seen. Like playing a game of hide and seek, but the seeker doesn't know you're even hiding. They decide to send twelve spies into the land. Each of them represents a different part of God's people. They are putting together a plan on how to move into the Promised Land.

What do you think the spies will find in the Promised Land?

*and see what the land is, and whether the people who dwell in it
are strong or weak, whether they are few or many*
Numbers 13:18

The spies that go into the Promised Land make note of three things: the people that live there, the places they live in, and the land they live on. Each of these will be important for them to share with God's people. The first thing they take note of is the people. They want to find out if they are strong or weak people.

Because the people already live there, when God's people come in, it will probably cause a fight. People don't like to share their homes and land. So, the spies want to know if they can win the battle before the fight begins.

Should God's people fight to take the land?

*and whether the land that they dwell in is good or bad, and
whether the cities that they dwell in are camps or strongholds,*
Numbers 13:19

The second thing the spies were to look into was the place where the people lived. They were supposed to look and see if they lived in big cities with massive walls or small towns with no protection. For example, when they wanted to see if the people were strong or weak, they wanted to know if the cities were strong or weak, too.

All of this would help them put together a strategy. When you play sports, you try to make a strategy based on the other teams' strengths and weaknesses. The spies were looking for strengths and weaknesses.

What kinds of strengths and weaknesses do you think they'll find?

*"And whether the land is rich or poor, and whether there are trees
in it or not. Be of good courage and bring some of the fruit of the
land." Now the time was the season of the first ripe grapes.*
Numbers 13:20

The last thing they were supposed to look at was the land. In the Bible, most people lived by gardening and farming. They made money and made dinner the same way, through their crops. So, it was important to know if the land they were looking at had good crops.

If it didn't have good crops, it wouldn't be a good place to live. But how did God describe the land before they got there? He called it a land flowing with milk and honey. If God's promise is true about the land, then it should be a perfect place for them to live.

Why was it important for the land to be good?

And they told him, "We came to the land to which you sent us.
It flows with milk and honey, and this is its fruit."
Numbers 13:27

Has anyone ever told you, "I've got bad news and good news. Which do you want first?" When people ask me that, I always say, "Give me the bad news first so the good news can cheer me up." In this verse, the spies give the good news first.

In the Promised Land, they find massive grapes and wonderful fruit to eat. They tell everyone that it is exactly what God promised. It is a land flowing with milk and honey. God has been faithful. He led them across the Red Sea. He led them through the wilderness. Now, they stand at the front door of the greatest place to live. This is good news!

What could turn this into bad news?

However, the people who dwell in the land are strong, and
the cities are fortified and very large. And besides, we saw the
descendants of Anak there.
Numbers 13:28

God made two major promises about the Promised Land. He said that it would be a land flowing with milk and honey. Check. That's true. But God also promised that He would go before them in every battle. This means that they will have to fight their way into the Promised Land. Check again.

The bad news is that the second promise is true. The people who currently live in the Promised Land are strong, and the cities they live in have huge, strong walls. The fights they are about to get into will not be easy to win. If God's people are going to make it, they will have to trust what God said. He will go before them into battle.

Would you be scared to go into the Promised Land?

DAY 135: CALEB'S COURAGE

*But Caleb quieted the people before Moses and said, "Let us go up
at once and occupy it, for we are well able to overcome it."*
Numbers 13:30

I have never been a brave friend. Some people just have that courage built into them. Men and women like that become firefighters, policemen, or members of the military. Caleb, one of the spies in our stories, was a brave man. He would have made a great firefighter.

But Caleb's courage was not in his strength. He didn't tell Israel to follow him, and he would take care of it. Caleb's courage came from Caleb's God. He knew the promise that God would go before Him. He knew that God had conquered armies for them in the past. So Caleb trusted God, and that gave him courage.

When you're scared, what can you do to get courage?

DAY 136: THE SPIES' FEAR

*And there we saw the Nephilim (the sons of Anak, who come
from the Nephilim), and we seemed to ourselves like grasshoppers,
and so we seemed to them.*
Numbers 13:33

Caleb was outnumbered. Remember, 12 spies went into the Promised Land to scope it out. They all saw the same thing. They saw the good land. They saw the scary people that lived there. But unlike Caleb, the other spies were overwhelmed by the scary people.

They said that they were like grasshoppers compared to the people who lived there. This meant that the people in the Promised Land looked like giants to them. Instead of trusting God and gaining courage, they let fear control them. Fear led them to the sin of disobedience.

How can fear cause us to sin?

And they said to one another, "Let us choose a leader and go back to Egypt."
Numbers 14:4

Have you ever had a teacher that you didn't like? Maybe you've had a bad day with your teacher, and you wish you didn't have them anymore. God's people are so frustrated with Moses and scared of the people in the Promised Land they demand two things. They want a new leader, and they want to go back to Egypt.

Being frustrated and scared can cause us to do all kinds of crazy things. They think that going back to slavery would be better than trusting God in the Promised Land. The next time you're frustrated and scared, stop and breathe for a minute. Take time to remind yourself that God is in control and you can trust Him.

Why do we make bad choices when we're frustrated?

If the Lord delights in us, he will bring us into this land and give
it to us, a land that flows with milk and honey.
Numbers 14:8

Most children in the world have parents who love them. As a parent, I know what that love feels like. I love to show my kids that I love them by getting them little gifts. Seeing the smile that comes on their face with a milkshake or a new toy is incredible. I delight in them in that way.

The Bible says that God delights in us. This means that it brings Him joy to see us happy. He wants to provide for us. He wants to be there for us. Since this is true, God's people shouldn't fear going into the land that is filled with battles. God delights in them. He will take care of them.

Why does God delight in us?

*Only do not rebel against the Lord. And do not fear the people
of the land, for they are bread for us. Their protection is removed
from them, and the Lord is with us; do not fear them.*
Numbers 14:9

We are all tempted to be rebels. If you've seen a button with a sign that says, "Do not push," then you've probably felt the temptation to rebel. That feeling of ignoring the sign and pushing the button is rebellion building up inside of us. In a way, it's a natural thing for us.

But this natural thing that seems small sometimes can be big and sinful at other times. God's people are tempted to rebel against Him. It was His command to go into the Promised Land, but they were too scared to do that. They wanted to rebel and run away. God calls them and us not to rebel. He wants us to trust Him even when it's scary.

Have you ever rebelled against God?

DAY 140: PRAYER FOR FORGIVENESS

*Please pardon the iniquity of this people, according to the
greatness of your steadfast love, just as you have forgiven this
people, from Egypt until now.*
Numbers 14:19

We are told to pray in a lot of different ways in the Bible. Just a few days ago, we talked about how we are supposed to pray for healing. Some prayers are just prayers of thanksgiving and adoration. Other times, you pray for God's help in a difficult situation.

Another thing we can pray for is for forgiveness. This means that we ask God to forgive us for our sins. The Bible promises that if we confess our sins, then God is faithful and just to forgive us of our sins. Because of what Jesus did for us, we can always know that God forgives us.

How does it feel to know God will always forgive you?

But truly, as I live, and as all the earth shall be filled with the
glory of the Lord,
Numbers 14:21

I don't like arts and crafts. I'm not very good at it, and it always makes a mess. The one art supply that I despise is glitter. I cannot stand it for one reason. It gets everywhere. No matter how careful you are or how little you spill, once it's out of its container, it goes all over the place. In a matter of seconds, it covers the room.

God says that one day, His glory will be like untamed glitter. It will fill the whole earth. One day, when Jesus comes back and begins to live on this earth again, we will see the bright glory of God fill every dark crack. We won't need the sun because He will be everywhere.

What do you think God's glory will look like?

Shall see the land that I swore to give to their fathers.
And none of those who despised me shall see it.
Numbers 14:23

When I was a kid, I was scared to go on roller coasters. It took a long time for me to build up the courage to get on my first ride. There is nothing wrong with being scared sometimes. But there are some consequences for it. If you're too scared to get on a roller coaster, the consequence is that you don't get to enjoy riding the roller coaster.

God's people were too scared to go into the Promised Land. So, God's punishment was a natural consequence. They were not allowed to go in. God doomed them to wander in the wilderness for 40 more years before they got to try again. Whatever you're scared of, trust God. Otherwise, you may not get to the blessing of conquering fear.

What fear are you facing?

*But my servant Caleb, because he has a different spirit and has
followed me fully, I will bring into the land into which he went,
and his descendants shall possess it.*
Numbers 14:24

Do you remember courage, Caleb? God did, too. Even though the other eleven spies were too scared to go into the Promised Land, Caleb wasn't. He trusted that God would protect them. So, when the rest of God's people were punished because of their fear, Caleb was rewarded for his faith.

Caleb was told that he and his family would be able to go into the Promised Land one day and live there. God would keep His promise to them because they trusted Him to the end. We can trust God to the very end. Every promise God has made, He will keep. We don't need to doubt Him.

Why do some people doubt God?

*According to the number of the days in which you spied out the
land, forty days, a year for each day, you shall bear your iniquity
forty years, and you shall know my displeasure.'*
Numbers 14:34

There is a saying in the Bible that describes how the laws work. It goes like this. An eye for an eye and a tooth for a tooth. In other words, if you break someone's ball, then you have to give them a ball. If someone throws your sandwich on the ground, then they have to give you a sandwich. It's fair.

God's punishment is based on this idea. An eye for an eye and a tooth for a tooth. The punishment fits the crime. For each day they wandered and then rebelled, they earned a year's punishment. When you count it all up, that equals 40 years of more wandering they had to endure. God is a just God.

Why does justice matter?

*Do not go up, for the Lord is not among you, lest you be struck
down before your enemies.*
Numbers 14:42

Has this ever happened to you? Your parents come into your room and tell you to clean it up. You don't clean it right away. You keep on playing. So they come back in the room and say that you have to clean it now or you'll be grounded. What happens if you don't clean it right then? They come back in and say that you're grounded.

Have you ever tried to scramble to clean it really quickly after they grounded you? Does that get you out of trouble? Most likely not. It's too little, too late. God's people did this. God said that their punishment was wandering in the wilderness, so they tried to rush into the Promised Land. It was too little, too late.

When have you done too little, too late?

*But if you sin unintentionally, and do not observe all these
commandments that the Lord has spoken to Moses,*
Numbers 15:22

It is impossible to be perfect. Drawing a perfect circle by hand feels impossible, but it's not technically impossible. Bowling a perfect game feels impossible, but people have done it. When it comes to being perfect, without sin, it's truly impossible. We cannot do it. One of the main reasons is that we sin without even realizing it sometimes.

The Bible calls these unintentional sins. Even unintentional sins are held against us because God's law requires true perfection. That's truly impossible. This is why we all truly need Jesus. He was completely perfect and never even unintentionally sinned. How amazing is that!

Can you think of a time when you unintentionally sinned?

And it shall be a tassel for you to look at and remember all the
commandments of the Lord, to do them, not to follow after your
own heart and your own eyes, which you are inclined to whore after.
Numbers 15:39

I am getting old. One of the things that comes with getting old is getting forgetful. There are times I'll forget why I walked into a room or that my glasses are on my head. I've even forgotten how old I am before. Have you ever forgotten something?

God knows that we can be forgetful. So, He tells us to put reminders around ourselves so that we won't forget. In this verse, God tells them to put tassels on their clothes. Each tassel represents something they need to remember about God. We can do this too. Think about what you can use to remind yourself about God.

What can you use to remind yourself about God?

I am the Lord your God, who brought you out of the land of
Egypt to be your God: I am the Lord your God.
Numbers 15:41

It is easy to forget little things like where you put your toy or bookbag. It's hard to forget big things like your own name or who your parents are. God's people forget a big thing. They forget who their God is.

The reason they forget Him is because they don't talk to Him in prayer. They don't listen to Him by reading His word. They aren't doing all of the things He tells them to do. We can be forgetful of God, too. When we're scared or proud, we can forget how He is involved in it all. Be careful that you don't forget that He is the Lord your God.

Why do we forget God sometimes?

They assembled themselves together against Moses and against Aaron and said to them, "You have gone too far! For all in the congregation are holy, every one of them, and the Lord is among them. Why then do you exalt yourselves above the assembly of the Lord?"

Numbers 16:3

The last of the Ten Commandments is so important. Do you remember what it says? It says that we should not covet. That means that we should not keep a big desire for what someone else has. Sometimes, we call this jealousy, too. We can be jealous of what other people have or what they get to do.

Korah and his friends were jealous of Moses. They coveted his power and position as the leader of God's people. If they were the leaders, they would not do what Moses did. They would do their own thing. Little do they know that this jealousy is going to become a big problem for them.

What have you been jealous about?

And he said to Korah and all his company, "In the morning the Lord will show who is his, and who is holy, and will bring him near to him. The one whom he chooses he will bring near to him."

Numbers 16:5

Dogs can't talk. They can bark and point to communicate, but they can't talk. So, if you found a lost dog and two people came up to you and said that the dog was theirs, how can you figure out the truth? You can't just ask the dog.

One way you could do it is to let the dog go. He will go to the person he knows before he goes to the one he doesn't. Moses and Korah are arguing over who should be the leader of God's people. So Moses said, "We'll let God decide. He will show us who is His leader in the morning." Moses was confident that God had chosen him for this.

Why was Moses confident that he was the chosen leader?

*Then Korah assembled all the congregation against them at
the entrance of the tent of meeting. And the glory of the Lord
appeared to all the congregation.*
Numbers 16:19

I used to act in plays. There is a wonderful moment at the beginning of the play when the curtains are closed, and everyone is waiting for the play to begin. Sometimes, a person will come out and welcome everyone and introduce the play. Then the lights will dim. Then, the best part happens. The curtains are pulled back, and the beautiful scenery is revealed.

Korah and Moses and all the people of Israel were at the tent of meeting that morning. Then God's glory was revealed there. It was like the curtains had been drawn back, and the people got to see the beautiful presence of God.

How would seeing God's glory make you feel?

*But if the Lord creates something new, and the ground opens its
mouth and swallows them up with all that belongs to them, and
they go down alive into Sheol, then you shall know that these men
have despised the Lord.*
Numbers 16:30

Sin is described in a lot of ways in the Bible. Each way tells us a little more about what God thinks about sin. In this verse, he calls the sin of Korah despising the Lord. Do you know what the word despise means? It's a powerful word. It's a really strong word for the word hate. To despise someone means that you hate them.

When we sin, we show God that we hate Him. That's hard to think about. Why does God think that way? Because God loves us so much and knows the best thing for us. He wants us to love Him in return. So when we sin, we choose a path that God knows is not good for us and is not loving to Him.

Why is a sin called despising God?

And as soon as he had finished speaking all these words,
the ground under them split apart.
Numbers 16:31

There are great movies out there about natural disasters. There are ones about hurricanes and twisters. There are others about great floods. But I don't think one exists that talks about what happens in this verse sub-scripture. In this verse, the ground splits apart and swallows up the people. It is different from an earthquake. The earthquake would just leave a crack. This one divides, swallows, and seals itself back up.

This was the judgment of God against Cora and his rebellion. God made it clear that the leader that he wanted for his people was Moses. He would not tolerate anyone trying to take over. This is a word of warning for us. In the areas that we are not in charge, we must trust that God has put the right person in charge.

What areas are you not in charge of?

As for the censers of these men who have sinned at the cost of their
lives, let them be made into hammered plates as a covering for the
altar, for they offered them before the Lord, and they became holy.
Thus they shall be a sign to the people of Israel.
Numbers 16:38

Part of the sinful act that led to man being swallowed up by the Earth was the misuse of censors. A censor was something that was used to start a fire that would burn incense. Incense is something that smells good. These people were burning strange fires, according to the Bible. This means that they were not burning the incense.

After the people were punished, God used the old censors as a sign of what would happen if they sinned in this way again. God had those melted down and added to the altar. Every time they offered a sacrifice, they would be reminded of what a good and bad offering is.

Why would God reuse the censors?

*And Moses said to Aaron, "Take your censer, and put fire on it
from off the altar and lay incense on it and carry it quickly to the
congregation and make atonement for them, for wrath has gone
out from the Lord; the plague has begun."*
Numbers 16:46

In everything that we do, God looks at three things. He looks at our hands. He looks at our hearts. And he looks at our head. All three of these things must be working together in the right way to please him. Just because we do the right thing with our hands does not mean that our hearts are motivated with the right motivations.

But when all of these three things work together, something wonderful happens. God is worshiped in the way that he wants to be worshiped. It is a sweet and perfect thing. And at the end of the day, it is a gift from God. No one can be perfect all the time, but we can all worship him by his grace.

Why does our heart motivation matter?

*And the staff of the man whom I choose shall sprout. Thus I will
make to cease from me the grumblings of the people of Israel,
which they grumble against you.*
Numbers 17:5

One of the big mysteries of the Bible is that God chooses his people. We don't know why he would choose any of us to do anything for him. We are all sinful. We all make mistakes. We will all disappoint him. And yet he still chooses us.

This should amaze us and cause us to worship him. We have nothing that we can offer him and nothing that we can do to help him. Why would he take the time to choose us? The answer must be that he simply loves us. He loves us not because we are such incredible people. He loves us simply because he loves us.

Do you feel chosen by God?

And the people of Israel said to Moses, "Behold, we perish,
we are undone, we are all undone."
Numbers 17:12

When I was in high school, we used to play pranks on one another. One of the pranks that we would play on one another is called TP someone's house. Basically, you would take a roll of toilet paper and throw it through the trees and over someone's home. When you throw it through the air, it comes undone. That leaves a web of paper all over the yard.

One of the ways that the Bible describes our sin is by saying that we are undone like a roll of toilet paper that has been thrown across the yard. We are a mess. And we need someone to come to clean us up and put us back together. Praise God Jesus does that for us.

Why are we called undone?

Moreover, you shall speak and say to the Levites, 'When you take
from the people of Israel the tithe that I have given you from them
for your inheritance, then you shall present a contribution from it
to the Lord, a tithe of the tithe.".
Numbers 18:26

If you have gone to church for a long time, then you have heard of something called a tithe. Maybe you have heard your parents talk about taxes? That is similar to what a tithe is. A tithe is 10%. So when God asked people to give a tithe, he asked them to give 10% of what they had.

This system is how God provided for the people who worked in the sanctuary. Because they had no other way of getting a job or making money, they relied on people to give them part of what they had made. Still, the reason local churches can do ministry is because people give a percentage of what they make.

How can you give to the church?

*"Take the staff, and assemble the congregation, you and Aaron
your brother, and tell the rock before their eyes to yield its water.
So you shall bring water out of the rock for them and give drink
to the congregation and their cattle."*
Numbers 20:8

God has provided for his people in some miraculous ways. But here they are again in need of water. And here God goes again, providing them with water from a rock. God tells Moses simply to speak to the rock, and water will come forward.

Last time, God told him to strike the rock with his staff. But this time, God is showing Jus how powerful he can be. This time, he says, simply speak to the rock, and you'll get the same effect. Just like God spoke all things into creation, he gave Moses the ability to speak and have water come flowing from the rock.

How powerful must God be to speak and make things happen?

*And the Lord said to Moses and Aaron, "Because you did not believe in
me, to uphold me as holy in the eyes of the people of Israel, therefore you
shall not bring this assembly into the land that I have given them."*
Numbers 20:12

Moses was getting frustrated with God's people. By the time he made it to the rock that he was supposed to speak to, he was angry. In his frustration, he hit the rock with the staff like he did last time. But this time, he hit the rock twice. This was wrong in two ways. First, God did not tell Moses to strike the rock. God told him just to speak to it. Second, he acted out of anger. That is no way to obey God.

And so God punishes Moses because he was not able to trust God and follow his commands. Moses will endure the same punishment that the rest of Israel has to endure. He will not be able to enter into the promised land. He will have to wander through the wilderness And die outside of the promised land.

Why can we not obey God while being angry?

*Please let us pass through your land. We will not pass through
field or vineyard, or drink water from a well. We will go along
the King's Highway. We will not turn aside to the right hand or
to the left until we have passed through your territory.*
Numbers 20:17

God's people were back on the road again. Their long journey home had just gotten longer. In fact, right as they were about to enter the promised land, they had to turn around. Because of their sin, the guy would not let them in. And so they are destined to wander the desert For 40 more years. This means that they will find enemies for 40 years in the wilderness.

The posture of God's people is peace. They do not want to fight anybody. They do not want to cause trouble. That is a good and godly way to go about life. We should be people who attempt peace on all occasions.

How can you be a peacemaker today?

*Thus Edom refused to give Israel passage through his territory,
so Israel turned away from him.*
Numbers 20:21

it was a big deal for Israel to pass through someone's city. Israel was made up 1000s of people and all of their cattle. They had a whole lotta stuff, and they caused a lot of commotion when they came through. It is no wonder that the people they found in the wilderness did not want them to come through their cities.

Made life hard for God's people. They needed places to stop and rest. They needed cities to get supplies from. But they were being out because of their size. Along the way, God's people would be getting more and more frustrated that they had not made it home to the promised land yet. They all desire to go back to Egypt, and slavery is going to creep back up.

How can you welcome people into your home?

*And Moses stripped Aaron of his garments and put them on
Eleazar his son. And Aaron died there on the top of the mountain.
Then Moses and Eleazar came down from the mountain.*
Numbers 20:28

Moses and Aaron were a good team for the most part. They helped each other out in difficult situations. But Aaron was not a perfect leader. He was not a great priest. He made a lot of mistakes. Sadly, at the end of his life, his mistakes were so great that he had to be stripped of his title.

Moses took the priest's garments from him and gave them to another. This meant that Aaron could not be called the high priest any longer. He no longer had that title. This would be such a sad way to end your life. The title that you worked so hard to earn when you were younger was taken from him at the end. The destruction that sin brings does not care if you are young or old.

How can you lose things because of sin?

DAY 164: MOURNING

*And when all the congregation saw that Aaron had perished,
all the house of Israel wept for Aaron thirty days.*
Numbers 20:29

For the majority of my childhood, I had the same pastor. His name was Pastor Paul. He was funny and kind. And he would always wear his pants high up. I never quite understood why he wore his pants that way. But we loved him because he loved us so well. It was a really sad day when Pastor Paul died.

God's people are really sad in this verse. Their pastor, Aaron, the priest, had just died. Even though he was stripped of his title in the end, everybody still loved him. Everybody still missed him and needed to mourn for him. It is a good thing for us to mourn and weep when we lose someone. Never feel bad about crying over someone you love.

Have you ever lost someone important to you?

And the Lord heeded the voice of Israel and gave over the
Canaanites, and they devoted them and their cities to destruction.
So the name of the place was called Hormah.
Numbers 21:3

There is a lot of irony in these verses. God's people were scared of fighting. That's why they didn't go into the promised land. But what are they doing now? As they wander around the wilderness, they are going to fight. Sadly, all of this fighting is not going to get them what they need.

But God does not let them lose all of their battles. He still cares about them. He is still going to go before them and fight on their behalf. It is the grace of God that allows them to win this fight against the can. He gives them everything they need, even when they are disobedient to him. What a gracious God we serve.

Why does God keep fighting for His people?

Then the Lord sent fiery serpents among the people,
and they bit the people, so that many people of Israel died.
Numbers 21:6

Grumbling, grumbling, and more grumbling. This is what God's people do in the wilderness. Just like they did on the way to the promised land, they will continue to do so as they wander around outside of it. And God will continue to bring discipline to them. This time, he sends fiery serpents among his people. When they are bitten, they get sick and die.

I hate snakes. So, this would have been a really scary punishment for me. But God will not leave them without hope. In the next section that you read tomorrow, you'll see God's plan for salvation, even in their punishment.

Where else in the Bible is a snake the enemy of God's people?

*And the Lord said to Moses, "Make a fiery serpent and set it on a
pole, and everyone who is bitten, when he sees it, shall live."*
Numbers 21:8

The remedy for the snake bites is interesting. God does not send an anti-dote or medicine. He simply tells Moses to make a bronze snake and put it on a pole. Everyone who keeps their eye on the bronze snake will live. The core of this remedy is Faith. If people simply believe and trust that keeping their eye on the bronze snake will keep them safe, then they will be saved.

This is what it is to trust in Jesus. When we keep our eyes on him, then we will be saved, too. There is no special thing that we have to do. We don't have to pass a test. We simply have to trust that God's plan for salvation is Jesus and Jesus alone. By faith in him, we can be saved.

How are we saved?

DAY 168: WATER SONG

Then Israel sang this song: "Spring up, O well!—Sing to it!
Numbers 21:17

have you ever been to a waterfall? They are incredible to look out for. But waterfalls are not just beautiful to see. They are beautiful to listen to, too. It is wonderful to hear the sound of rushing water slamming against the rocks in the river below. God's people walk around in the desert to hear the sound of rushing water.

God, in his kindness, always provided water for them when they needed it. And so God's people are saying they praise God for this. The song was simple. They said spring up. Oh well. In other words, they wanted the Well to be filled with water. And they sang to God for it. And he provided.

Why can you sing to God today?

*And Israel took all these cities, and Israel settled in all the cities of
the Amorites, in Heshbon, and in all its villages.*
Numbers 21:25

Every summer, growing up, I had the opportunity to go to summer camp with my friends from church. We would pack our bags and get ready to spend an entire week in the mountains or at the beach. When we finally got down there and hauled all of our stuff inside our home for the week, we would set everything up. We would try to make our cabin feel as much like home as possible.

But no matter how much he tried. It never felt like home. It was always meant to be a temporary place to stay during the week. God's people are settling into a temporary home. They will not be completely content or happy while living there. They are still waiting for the day they can go into the promised land.

Why would the temporary home not make them happy?

*But the Lord said to Moses, "Do not fear him, for I have given him
into your hand, and all his people, and his land. And you shall do to
him as you did to Sihon king of the Amorites, who lived at Heshbon."*
Numbers 21:34

A really common phrase in the Bible is when God tells his people that he will give their enemies into their hands. What a strange way to describe victory in a battle. When you think about it, it makes sense. When you work with clay, you do so with your hands. The clay in your hands has to submit to what you want to do. It is not in charge.

So, when God says that he is going to give the enemies of God's people into their hands, he is saying he's gonna let them be in charge. The enemies cannot overcome them because they are just like clay in the hands of a potter.

How does this give God's people confidence?

"Come now, curse this people for me, since they are too mighty for me. Perhaps I shall be able to defeat them and drive them from the land, for I know that he whom you bless is blessed, and he whom you curse is cursed."
Numbers 22:6

Admitting that you need help can be hard. Pride can swell up in our hearts and not let us reach out when we need help. I can remember my son trying hard to build a house of cards only to see it fall before he was finished. Instead of asking for help, he faced defeat over and over again. It all ended in frustration and sadness.

The person in our verse learned to admit when he needed help. He said that his opponent was too mighty for him and that he needed God to fight for him. Our lives would be so much better if we were honest and admitted when we needed help.

Can you think of a time when you needed help?

God said to Balaam, "You shall not go with them. You shall not curse the people, for they are blessed."
Numbers 22:12

The story of Balaam and Balak is one of my favorites in the Bible. Spoiler alert: it ends with a talking donkey. That always makes me think of the movie Shrek. But before we get to talking animals, we have to start with the wicked king Balaam. Balak wanted Balaam to bless his nation.

God told Balaam that he could not bless that nation because they were enemies of God's people. This leads to a series of back-and-forth asking and rejecting. As long as Balak was an enemy of God's people, he would be an enemy of God.

Do you know of anyone who would be an enemy of God?

*But Balaam answered and said to the servants of Balak, "Though
Balak were to give me his house full of silver and gold, I could not
go beyond the command of the Lord my God to do less or more."*
Numbers 22:18

I am a die-hard Denver Broncos fan. In 1998, I watched as they won the Super Bowl. I jumped on the bandwagon then and never got off. Nothing can convince me to change my favorite team. Even now, they are not a good team anymore, but I cheer for them anyway. I am loyal to them.

Balaam was loyal to God. Balak was willing to give him all kinds of money if he would just bless his nation. But Balaam said that no amount of money could change his mind. He would only say and do what God told him to say and do.

When have you stuck to your position like this?

*Then the Lord opened the mouth of the donkey, and she said to Balaam,
"What have I done to you, that you have struck me these three times?"*
Numbers 22:28

I am a preacher. This means that I have the responsibility of standing before the church and proclaiming God's Word. It's a humbling and intimidating task. I'm already not comfortable talking in front of people. In addition, the pressure of speaking on behalf of God can feel too much.

But then I remember this story. God spoke through a donkey. If God can do that, then surely He can speak through me, too. When God wants to speak, nothing will silence Him. Don't let fear keep you from speaking God's word to someone else.

Is there someone in your life who needs to hear God's Word?

*Then the Lord opened the eyes of Balaam, and he saw the angel of
the Lord standing in the way, with his drawn sword in his hand.
And he bowed down and fell on his face.*
Numbers 22:31

One of the characters in the Bible that pops up from time to time is called "the angel of the Lord." It's possible that each time this comes up, it is a different angel. But it is more likely that it is the same one. He tends to do the same thing every time.

Imagine how surprised Balaam would have been on this donkey ride. Not only did the donkey speak to him, his eyes were opened to see an angel standing right in front of him. There are angels all around us. We should thank God for sending them to protect us.

What do you think the angel of the Lord looked like?

*And Balak said to Balaam, "What have you done to me? I took you to
curse my enemies, and behold, you have done nothing but bless them."*
Numbers 23:11

Jesus taught His disciples to "let their 'yes' be 'yes' and their 'no' be 'no.'" This means He taught them to keep their word. If they say "yes," they will do something, then they ought to do it. If they said "no," then they shouldn't do it. Balaam put that into practice.

Balak tried to twist his arm and force him to bless his nation. But Balaam refused and pronounced a curse on them instead. He was a man of his word. We should be, too. Our friends and family should be able to trust what we say.

Why is it important to keep your word?

And Balak said to Balaam, "Come now, I will take you to another place.
Perhaps it will please God that you may curse them for me from there."
Numbers 23:27

Do you know the definition of insanity? It is doing the same thing over and over again and expecting different results. Imagine making a set of paper wings and trying to use them to fly. What will happen the first time you jump off of your roof with them? You'll crash to the ground. That's not a good choice, but it's not insane.

An insane choice would be to jump ten more times, expecting to fly the next one. Balak is going insane. He keeps trying to force Balaam to bless his people. But Balaam will continue to pronounce curses and judgments.

Why do you think Balak kept trying?

He crouched, he lay down like a lion and like a lioness; who will rouse him
up? Blessed are those who bless you, and cursed are those who curse you.
Numbers 24:9

In Balaam's curse of Balak's nation, he describes God as a lion or a lioness. A lion is known for its strength. A lioness is known for her hunting ability. Balaam is saying that God is a strong and mighty hunter. You cannot force Him to do anything. If you pick a fight with Him, you better be prepared to lose.

We may think we don't pick fights with God. But if we think about it, we will find out that we do. Any time that we disobey God's commands, we are picking a fight. It's a fight we will not win. For our good and His glory, let's follow all He says for us to do.

What animal would you compare God to?

*I see him, but not now; I behold him, but not near: a star shall
come out of Jacob, and a scepter shall rise out of Israel; it shall
crush the forehead of Moab and break down all the sons of Sheth.*
Numbers 24:17

A star and a scepter. These two things are pictures of what Jesus will be like. He is what this verse is talking about. He will be like a star in that everyone will look up and see Him for what He is. One day, when He returns, the skies will be filled with His light, and all will know.

The second picture is of a scepter. A scepter is a rod that a king would hold. It was an object of power and authority. When Jesus returns, He will come as a powerful king who has all authority in Heaven and on earth. He is our coming king.

Are you ready for Jesus to return?

*So Israel yoked himself to Baal of Peor. And the anger of the Lord
was kindled against Israel.*
Numbers 25:3

Most likely, you've never seen a yoke before. Unless you grew up on a farm that uses cattle instead of tractors, yokes are foreign to you. Let me explain what they are. A yoke is a wooden bar that lies across the backs of two animals. Two animals that are yoked together can work together to pull a wagon.

God is saying that His people should not be yoked to another god. They shouldn't be connected and should not work together. If we follow another god, we should expect the anger of God to be kindled against us, too. Our God works alone with His people.

Why should we not be yoked with another god?

*Phinehas the son of Eleazar, son of Aaron the priest, has turned
back my wrath from the people of Israel, in that he was jealous
with my jealousy among them, so that I did not consume the
people of Israel in my jealousy.*
Numbers 25:11

There are two words that any Christian needs to know. They are zealous and jealous. They sound the same, but they have different meanings. To be zealous means that you are passionate about something. Bakers are zealous about bread, and contractors are zealous about building.

To be jealous means to be protective over what you're passionate about. If a baker finds out that another baker makes better bread than him, then he would be jealous of him. God calls us to be zealous and jealous of Him. We should be so passionate about our love for Him that we would call others to love Him, too.

How can you be zealous for God this week?

*And it shall be to him and to his descendants after him the
covenant of a perpetual priesthood, because he was jealous for his
God and made atonement for the people of Israel.*
Numbers 25:13

The perpetual priesthood is one of the greatest promises the believer can find in the Bible. A priest was a man of God who would offer sacrifices on behalf of the people. Because of what the priest did, the people could know that they were forgiven by God. God says He will keep a priest for His people forever. We can always know where we stand before God.

Jesus is the ultimate answer to this. He is our high priest forever. Because He died and rose again, we can be confident that the forgiveness He offers lasts forever. We never have to worry about how God feels about us. We know for sure.

Why do we need a perpetual priesthood?

This was the list of the people of Israel, 601,730.
Numbers 26:51

Some parts of the Bible are boring to read. Let's be honest. The Book of Numbers got its name for a reason. There are a bunch of numbers in it. Most of them are numbers that came from a census. A census is where you count how many people live in a certain place.

When God's people counted themselves, they found that there were 601,730 of them. That's huge! It's a fulfillment of one of God's promises, too. God told Abraham near the beginning of the Bible that He would make Abraham into a great nation. And what has He done? He kept His word, so don't skip the boring parts of the Bible. They are powerful when you see God's faithfulness in them.

How many people live in the city that you live in?

The land shall be divided by lot according to the names of the
tribes of their fathers.
Numbers 26:55

After counting all the people, God gave instructions on how the land should be divided among the tribes of Israel. This land was the Promised Land, the place God had been leading them to for so long. But it wasn't just a random division. It was done by lot, meaning God decided where each tribe would live.

This might seem like just a detail, but it's another example of how God is in control of everything. Even when it comes to where we live, God has a plan. He knows what's best for each of us, and He places us exactly where we need to be.

Have you ever thought about why you live where you do?

The daughters of Zelophehad were right. You shall give them
possession of an inheritance among their father's brothers.
Numbers 27:7

Zelophehad had no sons, only daughters. In those days, only sons would inherit the land. But these daughters came to Moses and asked for their father's inheritance. God agreed with them, and they received land just like the sons would have.

This story shows that God values everyone, not just those who fit into certain categories. He listens to everyone, and He cares about justice. No one is overlooked by God. He sees you, He hears you, and He cares about what happens to you.

How can you stand up for what's right, like Zelophehad's daughters?

The Lord said to Moses, "Take Joshua the son of Nun, a man in
whom is the Spirit, and lay your hand on him."
Numbers 27:18

Moses had been leading the Israelites for a long time, but his journey was coming to an end. God told him to appoint Joshua as the next leader. Joshua had been with Moses through many tough times, and now he would be the one to lead the people into the Promised Land.

Leadership is important, but it's also important to know when to pass the torch to someone else. Moses obeyed God and trusted that Joshua would continue leading the people well. God has a plan for every leader, and He prepares the right person for the right time.

Who do you look up to as a leader, and why?

*You shall offer one lamb in the morning, and the other lamb you
shall offer at twilight.*
Numbers 28:4

God gave the Israelites specific instructions about daily offerings. Every day, they were to offer two lambs—one in the morning and one in the evening. These offerings were a way to show devotion to God and remind the people of their need for Him every day.

This daily rhythm of worship kept the people connected to God. Just like the Israelites, we can have daily habits that keep us close to God. It might be reading the Bible, praying, or something else that helps us remember to rely on God throughout the day.

What's something you can do every day to stay close to God?

DAY 188: FEAST OF TRUMPETS

It is a day for you to blow the trumpets.
Numbers 29:1

The Feast of Trumpets was a special day for the Israelites. They would blow trumpets as a way to gather the people and announce the beginning of a holy time. It was a day of rest and worship, where the people could remember all that God had done for them.

The sound of a trumpet is hard to ignore. It's loud and grabs your attention. In the same way, God wants to grab our attention. He wants us to stop what we're doing and focus on Him. The Feast of Trumpets reminds us to take time to listen to God and celebrate His goodness.

When was the last time you stopped and listened to God?

*If a man vows a vow to the Lord, or swears an oath to bind
himself by a pledge, he shall not break his word.*
Numbers 30:2

Making a promise to God is a serious thing. When someone made a vow to the Lord, they were expected to keep it. God takes our words seriously, and He wants us to be people who keep our promises. Whether it's a vow to God or a promise to someone else, it's important to follow through.

This teaches us about integrity—doing what you say you will do. It's not always easy, but it's something God values highly. When we keep our promises, we show that we are trustworthy and that we respect God and others.

What's a promise you've made that you need to keep?

*And they warred against Midian, as the Lord commanded Moses,
and killed every male.*
Numbers 31:7

God commanded the Israelites to go to war against Midian, and they were victorious. This wasn't just about winning a battle; it was about obeying God's command. The Israelites trusted God's guidance, and He gave them victory.

Sometimes, we face battles in life that seem tough. It could be a difficult situation or a challenge we don't know how to handle. But just like the Israelites, when we trust God and follow His guidance, He can give us victory over our challenges.

What battle are you facing right now?
How can you trust God to help you through it?

Take count of the plunder that was taken, both of man and of
beast, you and Eleazar the priest and the heads of the fathers'
houses of the congregation.
Numbers 31:26

After the Israelites won the battle against Midian, God gave them instructions on how to divide the spoils—everything they had taken in battle. The spoils were shared among the warriors and the rest of the Israelites and even given as offerings to the Lord. This division ensured that everyone benefited from the victory and that God was honored.

This teaches us about sharing and generosity. When God blesses us with something good, it's important to think about how we can share those blessings with others. Whether it's time, talent, or treasure, God loves a generous heart.

What's something good in your life that you can share with others?

Now the people of Reuben and the people of Gad had a very great
number of livestock. And they saw the land of Jazer and the land
of Gilead, and behold, the place was a place for livestock.
Numbers 32:1

The tribes of Reuben and Gad saw that the land of Jazer and Gilead was perfect for their livestock. Instead of crossing over into the Promised Land with the rest of Israel, they asked Moses if they could settle there. Moses agreed, but only if they promised to help the other tribes fight for the rest of the land first.

This story shows the importance of working together and supporting one another. Even though the Reubenites and Gadites found what they wanted, they didn't forget about their responsibilities to the rest of the community. We all have a part to play in helping each other reach our goals.

How can you help someone else achieve their goal?

*Thus the Lord has done to this place; to this day, you have seen
how He has walked with you.*
Numbers 32:10

As the Israelites approached the Promised Land, Moses reminded them of everything God had done for them. He had been with them through their struggles, provided for them, and led them every step of the way. Remembering God's faithfulness was key to trusting Him for the future.

It's easy to forget how much God has done when we're facing new challenges. But when we remember His faithfulness in the past, it gives us confidence to trust Him with what's ahead. God doesn't change; the same God who helped us before will help us again.

Can you think of a time when God was faithful to you?

This shall be your land as defined by its border all around.
Numbers 34:12

God gave the Israelites clear instructions about the boundaries of the land they were to inherit. He defined their territory, giving them a specific place to call their own. Knowing their boundaries helped the Israelites understand their responsibility and the area they were meant to care for.

God gives us boundaries, too—not just physical ones, but moral and spiritual ones as well. These boundaries help us know how to live in a way that honors Him. They protect us and keep us on the right path.

What boundaries has God set for your life, and how do they help you?

*Then you shall select cities to be cities of refuge for you, that the
man slayer who kills any person without intent may flee there.*
Numbers 35:11

God instructed the Israelites to set aside cities of refuge—places where someone who accidentally killed another person could go for safety. These cities were important because they provided protection and a fair trial, ensuring that justice was done.

The cities of refuge remind us that God cares about justice and mercy. He provides a way for us to be protected and to find refuge when we make mistakes. Jesus is our ultimate refuge, offering us safety and forgiveness when we come to Him.

Where do you turn when you need refuge?

*But if you do not drive out the inhabitants of the land from before
you, then those of them whom you let remain shall be as barbs in
your eyes and thorns in your sides, and they shall trouble you in
the land where you dwell.*
Numbers 33:55

As the Israelites prepared to enter the Promised Land, God warned them to drive out all the inhabitants of the land. If they allowed any to remain, those people would cause trouble and lead the Israelites away from God. This was a serious warning about the danger of compromise.

Compromise might seem like an easy solution, but it can lead to problems down the road. When it comes to our relationship with God, it's important to stay true to His commands and not let anything distract us or pull us away from Him.

Is there anything in your life that's tempting you to compromise?

These are the stages of the people of Israel, when they went out
of the land of Egypt by their companies under the leadership of
Moses and Aaron.
Numbers 33:1

The Book of Numbers recounts the journey of the Israelites from Egypt to the Promised Land, listing the places they camped along the way. As they looked back on their journey, it became clear that a new generation was about to enter the land. The old generation, who had doubted God, had passed away, and now their children were ready to receive the promise.

This new generation had a fresh start and a chance to trust God in ways their parents hadn't. It's a reminder that each new generation has the opportunity to follow God with fresh faith and obedience.

How can you be part of a generation that trusts and follows God?

And the Lord spoke to Moses, saying, "Command the people
of Israel to give to the Levities some of the inheritance of their
possession as cities for them to dwell in.
Numbers 35:1-2

The Levites were set apart as the tribe responsible for serving in the Tabernacle and later the Temple. Since they didn't receive their territory like the other tribes, God commanded the Israelites to give them cities within their territories. This ensured that the Levites would be supported and could focus on their duties to God.

God provides for those who serve Him. He makes sure that they have what they need to fulfill their calling. It's also a reminder for us to support those who dedicate their lives to serving God and His people.

How can you support those who serve God in your community?

*The cities that you give to the Levities shall be the six cities of
refuge, where you shall permit the man slayer to flee, and in
addition to them you shall give forty-two cities.*
Numbers 35:6

The Levites were given a total of 48 cities throughout the territories of Israel, including six cities of refuge where someone who had accidentally killed another person could find safety. These cities served as places of justice, protection, and service to God.

The Levites didn't have a land inheritance like the other tribes because their inheritance was the Lord. They were spread throughout Israel to serve the people and maintain the spiritual health of the nation. This setup ensured that God's presence and teachings were accessible to everyone, no matter where they lived.

*Think about how God places people in your life to help guide you in your faith.
How can you show appreciation for those who help you grow spiritually?*

*What important decisions are you facing,
and how can you seek God's guidance in them?*

*If anyone kills a person, the murderer shall be put to death on the evidence of
witnesses. But no person shall be put to death on the testimony of one witness.*
Numbers 35:30

God's law provided clear guidelines for justice, especially regarding life and death situations. In the cities of refuge, someone accused of murder would have a fair trial. If there was enough evidence, the guilty party would be punished. However, God made sure that no one would be condemned based on just one witness. This law ensured that justice was fair and that the innocent were protected.

Justice is important to God, and He wants us to be fair in how we treat others. It's important to listen carefully, gather all the facts, and ensure that what we do is right in God's eyes.

*How can you practice fairness in your life,
especially when making decisions about others?*

DAY 201: NO RANSOM FOR A MURDERER

Moreover, you shall accept no ransom for the life of a murderer,
who is guilty of death, but he shall be put to death.
Numbers 35:31

God made it clear that the life of a murderer could not be ransomed. This means that someone guilty of taking a life could not pay money or offer anything else to avoid the penalty of death. This commandment showed the seriousness of taking a life and upheld the value of justice in Israel.

This teaches us that some things cannot be bought or exchanged. Justice, especially in serious matters, must be upheld. It also shows us that God values life greatly, and we should, too.

How does knowing that God values life influence the way you treat others?

DAY 202: THE LAND MUST BE CLEANSED

You shall not pollute the land in which you live, for blood pollutes
the land, and no atonement can be made for the land for the blood
that is shed in it, except by the blood of the one who shed it.
Numbers 35:33

God commanded the Israelites not to pollute the land with the shedding of innocent blood. The only way to cleanse the land after such a serious crime was for the guilty party to be punished. This shows how much God cares about the land and the people living in it. When justice was served, the land could be at peace.

This reminds us that our actions have consequences, not just for ourselves but for our communities and the places we live. God wants us to live in a way that brings peace and not harm to others.

What are some ways you can help keep your community safe and at peace?

*This is what the Lord commands concerning the daughters of
Zelophehad: Let them marry whom they think best, only they
shall marry within the clan of the tribe of their father.*
Numbers 36:6

God gave specific instructions about the marriage of female heirs, like the daughters of Zelophehad, to ensure that the land inheritance stayed within the tribe. This rule was put in place to preserve the inheritance and maintain the integrity of each tribe's portion in the Promised Land.

This story highlights the importance of honoring God's commands even in personal decisions like marriage. It's about making choices that align with God's will and preserve what He has given us.

*What important decisions are you facing,
and how can you seek God's guidance in them?*

*Every one of the people of Israel shall hold on to the inheritance of
the tribe of his fathers.*
Numbers 36:7

As the Israelites prepared to enter the Promised Land, God gave specific instructions to ensure that each tribe's inheritance remained within the tribe. This meant that land could not be permanently transferred to another tribe, preserving the identity and heritage of each tribe. The daughters of Zelophehad were allowed to marry within their tribe to keep their father's inheritance intact.

This teaches us the importance of preserving what God has given us. Whether it's our faith, our family, or our community, God wants us to value and protect the things He has entrusted to us.

What is something important in your life that you want to protect and preserve?

*These are the commandments and the rules that the Lord
commanded the people of Israel by Moses in the plains of
Moab by the Jordan at Jericho.*
Numbers 36:13

As the book of Numbers concludes, Moses gives the Israelites final instructions from the Lord. These commandments and rules were to guide them as they entered the Promised Land. Moses faithfully delivered God's word, knowing that it was vital for the Israelites to follow His commands if they were to succeed in the land God was giving them.

This reminds us that God's word is our guide in life. Following His instructions helps us live in a way that pleases Him and brings us blessings. Just as the Israelites needed God's word to succeed, we do too.

How do you make sure you're following God's word in your daily life?

*And you shall remember the whole way that the Lord your God
has led you these forty years in the wilderness, that he might
humble you, testing you to know what was in your heart,
whether you would keep his commandments or not.*
Deuteronomy 8:2

As the Israelites stood on the brink of the Promised Land, Moses reminded them of the past forty years. God had led them through the wilderness, humbling them and testing their hearts. These trials were meant to teach them dependence on God and obedience to His commands.

It's important to look back and remember how God has guided you through difficult times. These experiences shape your faith and prepare you for what's ahead.

How has God guided you through challenging times in your life?

DAY 207: MAN DOES NOT LIVE BY BREAD ALONE

*And he humbled you and let you hunger and fed you with manna,
which you did not know, nor did your fathers know, that he
might make you know that man does not live by bread alone, but
man lives by every word that comes from the mouth of the Lord.*
Deuteronomy 8:3

During their time in the wilderness, God provided the Israelites with manna, teaching them that their true sustenance came from Him. It wasn't just physical food that sustained them but God's word and presence in their lives.

This verse reminds us that our spiritual nourishment is even more important than our physical needs. We need God's word to guide and sustain us daily.

What steps can you take to make sure you're feeding on God's word every day?

DAY 208: DO NOT FORGET THE LORD

*Take care lest you forget the Lord your God by not keeping his
commandments and his rules and his statutes, which I command
you today.*
Deuteronomy 8:11

As the Israelites prepared to enter a land of plenty, Moses warned them not to forget the Lord in their prosperity. It's easy to rely on God in difficult times, but when things are going well, we can forget our dependence on Him. Moses urged the people to remember God's commandments and to continue following Him faithfully.

In times of blessing and abundance, it's important to keep God at the center of our lives. Remembering His commandments helps us stay grounded in our faith.

*How can you ensure that you remember God during
both the good times and the tough times?*

Know that in your heart that, as a man disciplines his son,
the Lord your God disciplines you.
Deuteronomy 8:5

Moses reminded the Israelites that the challenges they faced in the wilderness were a form of God's discipline, just as a father disciplines his children. This discipline wasn't meant to harm them but to teach them and help them grow in their relationship with God.

God's discipline in our lives is a sign of His love. He corrects us and guides us so that we can become more like Him.

How have you experienced God's discipline, and how has it helped you grow?

Beware lest you say in your heart, 'My power and the might of
my hand have gotten me this wealth.'
Deuteronomy 8:17

As the Israelites were about to enter a land flowing with abundance, Moses warned them against the sin of pride. He reminded them that it was God who gave them the power to prosper. Forgetting this could lead to self-reliance and turning away from God.

Pride can easily creep into our hearts, especially when we experience success. Remembering that all good things come from God keeps us humble and thankful.

What can you do to guard against pride in your life?

*You shall remember the Lord your God, for it is he who gives you
power to get wealth, that he may confirm his covenant that he
swore to your fathers, as it is this day.*
Deuteronomy 8:18

Moses reminded the Israelites that their ability to gain wealth and prosperity was a gift from God, not something they achieved on their own. God provided them with the means to prosper as part of His covenant with their forefathers. This was a reminder to stay humble and grateful, recognizing that every blessing comes from the Lord.

Wealth and success can easily lead to pride if we forget who the true source is. Remembering that God gives us the ability to achieve anything helps us stay grounded in our faith and purpose.

How can you express gratitude to God for the blessings in your life today?

*And if you forget the Lord your God and go after other gods and serve them
and worship them, I solemnly warn you today that you shall surely perish.*
Deuteronomy 8:19

Moses issued a stern warning to the Israelites about the dangers of forgetting God and turning to other gods. The consequences of abandoning their faith would be severe, leading to destruction and loss. This warning was meant to keep the people focused on their relationship with God and prevent them from straying into idolatry.

The temptation to put other things before God is always present, but the consequences of doing so are serious. Staying faithful to God and prioritizing Him above all else is crucial for our spiritual well-being.

What steps can you take to ensure that God remains the top priority in your life?

DAY 213: NOT BECAUSE OF YOUR RIGHTEOUSNESS

*Not because of your righteousness or the uprightness of your heart are
you going in to possess their land, but because of the wickedness of these
nations the Lord your God is driving them out from before you.*
Deuteronomy 9:5

Moses made it clear to the Israelites that they were not entering the Promised Land because of their righteousness but because of the wickedness of the nations that occupied it. God was fulfilling His promise to the forefathers, and it was His grace, not their merit, that led them to this point.

This reminds us that God's blessings in our lives are not earned by our righteousness but are gifts of His grace. We should always remain humble and grateful, recognizing that it's God's mercy that brings us to where we are.

How can you acknowledge God's grace in your life today?

DAY 214: A STIFF-NECKED PEOPLE

*Remember and do not forget how you provoked the Lord your
God to wrath in the wilderness. From the day you came out of
the land of Egypt until you came to this place, you have been
rebellious against the Lord.*
Deuteronomy 9:7

Moses reminded the Israelites of their history of rebellion against God, calling them a "stiff-necked people." Despite God's continuous provision and guidance, they often resisted His will and provoked His anger. This reminder was intended to keep them humble and aware of their need for repentance and obedience.

We, too, can be stubborn and resistant to God's leading in our lives. Reflecting on our past mistakes can help us remain humble and seek God's forgiveness, striving to follow His will more closely.

Are there areas in your life where you've been resistant to God's direction?

So I lay prostrate before the Lord for these forty days and forty
nights, because the Lord had said he would destroy you.
Deuteronomy 9:25

Moses interceded on behalf of the Israelites when God's anger burned against them due to their rebellion. For forty days and nights, he prayed and pleaded with God not to destroy the people. His intercession was an act of love and leadership, showing his deep care for the people despite their flaws.

Interceding in prayer for others is a powerful act of love. Just as Moses stood in the gap for the Israelites, we can pray for those around us, asking God to show mercy and grace in their lives.

Who can you intercede for in prayer today?

At the time the Lord said to me, 'Cut for yourself two tablets of stone like
the first, and come up to me on the mountain and make an ark of wood.'
Deuteronomy 10:1

After the Israelites broke the first tablets of the covenant by their disobedience, God graciously gave them a second set. Moses was instructed to bring two new tablets up the mountain, where God would inscribe His commandments once again. This act symbolized God's willingness to renew His covenant with a repentant people.

God's willingness to restore and renew His relationship with us, even after we fail, is a testament to His grace. No matter how many times we fall short, God is always ready to welcome us back and restore us.

How has God renewed His covenant with you after a time of failure?

And now, Israel, what does the Lord your God require of you, but to
fear the Lord your God, to walk in all his ways, to love him, to serve
the Lord your God with all your heart and with all your soul.
Deuteronomy 10:12

Moses laid out a simple yet profound call to the Israelites: fear God, walk in His ways, love Him, and serve Him with all your heart and soul. This was the essence of what God desired from His people—a wholehearted commitment to Him in every aspect of their lives.

God's requirements for us are the same today. He desires our complete devotion, love, and service. It's not about following a long list of rules but about living a life fully committed to God.

How can you show your love and devotion to God in your daily life?

Circumcise therefore the foreskin of your heart,
and be no longer stubborn.
Deuteronomy 10:16

Moses called the Israelites to "circumcise" their hearts, a metaphor for removing anything that hindered their relationship with God. It was a call to turn away from stubbornness and rebellion and to open their hearts fully to God's will.

In our lives, there may be attitudes, habits, or sins that harden our hearts and keep us from fully following God. We're called to cut away these barriers and allow God to transform us from the inside out.

What barriers are preventing you from fully surrendering to God?

*He executes justice for the fatherless and the widow,
and loves the sojourner, giving him food and clothing.*
Deuteronomy 10:18

Moses reminded the Israelites of God's heart for justice, particularly for the vulnerable—the fatherless, the widow, and the sojourner (foreigner). God's care for those on the margins of society was a model for how the Israelites were to treat others, especially those who were different or in need.

God's love extends to all people, regardless of their status or background. We're called to reflect His love by showing kindness and justice to those who are vulnerable and in need.

How can you show God's love to those who are vulnerable in your community?

*He is your praise. He is your God, who has done for you these
great and terrifying things that your eyes have seen.*
Deuteronomy 10:21

Moses reminded the Israelites that the Lord was their reason for praise. It was God who had performed great wonders before their eyes, leading them out of Egypt and through the wilderness. Their praise was to be directed to Him alone, acknowledging His power and faithfulness.

Our praise should always be centered on God, who has done great things in our lives. Remembering His past faithfulness inspires us to continue trusting and worshiping Him.

What great things has God done in your life that you can praise Him for today?

DAY 221: LOVE THE LORD YOUR GOD

*You shall therefore love the Lord your God and keep his charge,
his statutes, his rules, and his commandments always.*
Deuteronomy 11:1

Moses emphasized the importance of loving God and obeying His commandments. This love was not just about feelings but about action—keeping God's commands and living according to His ways. It was a reminder that true love for God is demonstrated through obedience.

Loving God isn't just something we say; it's something we show by how we live. Obedience to His commands is a reflection of our love and commitment to Him.

How can you show your love for God through your actions today?

DAY 222: TEACH THEM TO YOUR CHILDREN

*You shall teach them to your children, talking of them when you
are sitting in your house, and when you are walking by the way,
and when you lie down, and when you rise.*
Deuteronomy 11:19

Moses instructed the Israelites to diligently teach God's commands to their children. It was to be a continuous process, integrated into every aspect of daily life. This was crucial for passing down faith from one generation to the next and ensuring that God's ways were always remembered.

Teaching the next generation about God is one of the most important responsibilities we have. It's not just about formal lessons but about living out our faith in a way that our children can see and learn from.

What are some ways you can share your faith with the younger generation?

See, I am setting before you today a blessing and a curse: the blessing, if you obey the commandments of the Lord your God, which I command you today, and the curse, if you do not obey the commandments of the Lord your God.
Deuteronomy 11:26–28

Moses laid out a clear choice before the Israelites: obedience to God's commandments would bring blessings, while disobedience would result in curses. This stark contrast was meant to encourage the people to choose the path of obedience and life.

Our choices have consequences, and God gives us the freedom to choose. Choosing to follow His ways leads to blessings, while turning away from Him leads to difficulties. It's a daily decision to walk in obedience.

What choices are you making today that will lead to God's blessing in your life?

But you shall seek the place that the Lord your God will choose out of all your tribes to put his name and make his habitation there. There you shall go.
Deuteronomy 12:5

God instructed the Israelites to worship Him at the place He would choose rather than following their preferences. This place would be special, chosen by God for His presence to dwell. It was a call to worship God according to His direction, not their ideas.

Worship isn't about what's convenient or comfortable for us; it's about honoring God in the way He desires. Seeking God's will in how we worship helps us stay focused on Him and avoid distractions.

How can you align your worship with what God desires?

Take care that you be not ensnared to follow them, after they have been destroyed before you, and that you do not inquire about their gods, saying, "How did these nations serve their gods?–that I also may do the same."
Deuteronomy 12:30

Moses warned the Israelites not to be curious about the gods of the nations they were displacing. They were to avoid any temptation to follow those gods or adopt their practices. This was a protective measure to keep the Israelites faithful to the one true God.

Curiosity about things that lead us away from God can be dangerous. We need to guard our hearts and minds against influences that could draw us away from our faith and lead us into idolatry.

What steps can you take to guard your heart against anything that could lead you away from God?

*Everything that I command you, you shall be careful to do.
You shall not add to it or take from it.*
Deuteronomy 12:32

Moses gave a clear instruction to the Israelites: they were to follow God's commands exactly as given. They were not to add to or take away from His words. This was to ensure that their worship and obedience remained pure and true to God's will.

It's easy to want to adjust God's commands to fit our preferences or circumstances, but we're called to follow His Word faithfully. God's instructions are perfect and complete, and we should strive to obey them fully.

Are there areas in your life where you've been tempted to add to or take away from God's commands?

*If a prophet or a dreamer of dreams arises among you and gives
you a sign or a wonder, and the sign or wonder that he tells you
comes to pass, and if he says, 'Let us go after other gods,' which you
have not known, and let us serve them, you shall not listen to the
words of that prophet or that dreamer of dreams.*
Deuteronomy 13:1–3a

Moses warned the Israelites about false prophets who might perform signs and wonders but lead them to follow other gods. Even if the signs were impressive, if the message contradicted God's commands, the prophet was to be rejected. This was a test of the Israelites' loyalty to God.

Not everything that looks miraculous or powerful is from God. We must be discerning, testing everything against the truth of God's Word. If something or someone leads us away from God, we should turn away, no matter how convincing it might seem.

*How can you be discerning when faced with teachings or signs that
seem impressive but may not align with God's Word?*

*You are the sons of the LORD your God. You shall not cut
yourselves or make any baldness on your foreheads for the dead.
For you are a people holy to the LORD your God, and the LORD
has chosen you to be a people for his treasured possession, out of all
the peoples who are on the face of the earth.*
Deuteronomy 14:1–2

God called the Israelites to be set apart as His holy people. This meant that they were not to adopt the customs and practices of the surrounding nations, particularly those that were tied to pagan worship. As God's treasured possession, they were to live in a way that reflected their unique relationship with Him.

We, too, are called to be holy, set apart for God. This means living differently from the world around us, reflecting God's character and values in all we do.

In what ways can you live as someone who is set apart for God's purposes?

*You shall not eat any abomination. These are the animals you may
eat: the ox, the sheep, the goat...*
Deuteronomy 14:3-4

God provided specific dietary laws to the Israelites, instructing them on which animals were clean and could be eaten and which were unclean and to be avoided. These laws were part of what set the Israelites apart from other nations and served as a reminder of their call to holiness.

While we are no longer bound by these specific dietary laws, the principle of being mindful about what we consume—both physically and spiritually—still applies. We should be careful to fill our lives with things that are pure and pleasing to God.

*How can you be more mindful of what you consume,
both physically and spiritually?*

*At the end of every seven years you shall grant a release. And this
is the manner of the release: every creditor shall release what he
has lent to his neighbor. He shall not exact it of his neighbor, his
brother, because the LORD's release has been proclaimed.*
Deuteronomy 15:1-2

God instituted a year of release for the Israelites every seven years, during which debts were forgiven. This was a way of ensuring that no one was permanently burdened by debt and that the community could experience renewal and restoration.

God's command for a year of release teaches us about the importance of forgiveness and grace. We are called to forgive others, just as God has forgiven us, and to release the burdens that hold us and others down.

*Is there someone you need to forgive or something you need to let
go of to experience God's freedom and restoration?*

For there will never cease to be poor in the land. Therefore
I command you, 'You shall open wide your hand to your brother,
to the needy and to the poor, in your land.
Deuteronomy 15:11

God reminded the Israelites that poverty would always exist, and because of this, they were commanded to be generous and open-handed toward those in need. Generosity was to be a defining characteristic of God's people, reflecting His care and provision.

God calls us to be generous with what we have, knowing that everything we possess comes from Him. When we give to others, we're not just meeting physical needs but also demonstrating God's love and compassion.

How can you show generosity to someone in need today?

If your brother, a Hebrew man or a Hebrew woman, is sold
to you, he shall serve you six years, and in the seventh
year you shall let him go free from you.
Deuteronomy 15:12

God provided a law that after six years of service, a Hebrew servant was to be released in the seventh year. This law ensured that no one would be enslaved indefinitely and that freedom was always in sight. It was a reminder of God's deliverance and care for His people.

Freedom is a central theme in God's relationship with us. Just as He delivered Israel from slavery, He offers us freedom through Jesus Christ. We are called to live in that freedom and to help others experience it as well.

What does freedom in Christ mean to you,
and how can you help others find that freedom?

You shall keep the Feast of Unleavened Bread. Seven days you shall eat it with unleavened bread, the bread of affliction—for you came out of the land of Egypt in haste—that all the days of your life you may remember the day when you came out of the land of Egypt.
Deuteronomy 16:3

The Feast of Unleavened Bread was a time for the Israelites to remember their deliverance from Egypt. Eating unleavened bread, known as the bread of affliction, reminded them of the hardship they faced and the swiftness of God's deliverance.

Remembering what God has done in the past helps us trust Him for the future. The act of remembering is important in our faith journey, as it keeps us grounded in God's faithfulness.

What are some things God has done in your life that you need to remember and give thanks for?

Then you shall keep the Feast of Weeks to the Lord your God with the tribute of a freewill offering from your hand, which you shall give as the Lord your God blesses you.
Deuteronomy 16:10

The Feast of Weeks, also known as Pentecost, was a celebration of the harvest and a time to give thanks to God for His provision. It was marked by bringing a freewill offering to the Lord, given in proportion to how God had blessed each person.

Gratitude is a key part of our relationship with God. Recognizing His blessings and responding with a heart of thankfulness is a way to honor Him and keep our focus on His goodness.

How can you express your gratitude to God for the blessings in your life?

DAY 235: JUSTICE AND FAIRNESS

*You shall appoint judges and officers in all your towns that the
LORD your God is giving you, according to your tribes, and they
shall judge the people with righteous judgment. You shall not
pervert justice. You shall not show partiality, and you shall not
accept a bribe, for a bribe blinds the eyes of the wise and subverts
the cause of the righteous.*
Deuteronomy 16:18–19

God commanded the Israelites to establish a system of justice with judges who would uphold righteousness. They were warned not to pervert justice by showing partiality or accepting bribes, as these would corrupt the legal system and harm the community.

Justice and fairness are important to God, and He calls us to uphold these values in our lives. We are to treat others with integrity, standing against corruption and partiality.

*In what ways can you practice justice and fairness
in your interactions with others?*

DAY 236: WORSHIPING ONLY THE TRUE GOD

*You shall not plant any tree as an Asherah beside the altar of the
LORD your God that you shall make. And you shall not set
up a pillar, which the LORD your God hates.*
Deuteronomy 16:21–22

God commanded the Israelites not to mix the worship of false gods with the worship of Him. The Asherah poles and pillars were symbols of pagan worship, and God made it clear that His people were to worship Him alone, without any compromise.

God desires our complete devotion. We cannot mix our faith with things that dishonor Him. Our worship should be pure and focused solely on God, without distractions or false idols.

*Are there any "idols" in your life that might
be taking your focus away from God?*

*The prophet who presumes to speak a word in my name that I
have not commanded him to speak, or who speaks in the name
of other gods, that same prophet shall die.*
Deuteronomy 18:20

God warned the Israelites about false prophets who claimed to speak in His name but were not truly sent by Him. The penalty for such deception was severe because it led people away from the truth and into error.

We must be careful to discern whether the messages we hear are truly from God. True prophets and teachers will always align with God's Word and lead us closer to Him, not away from Him.

How can you discern whether a message or teaching is truly from God?

*The Lord your God will raise up for you a prophet like me from
among you, from your brothers—it is to him you shall listen.*
Deuteronomy 18:15

Moses foretold the coming of a prophet like him, whom the people were to listen to. This prophecy ultimately pointed to Jesus, the greatest prophet who would bring God's message of salvation and lead His people to the truth.

Jesus is the fulfillment of this promise. He is the ultimate prophet, priest, and king. We are called to listen to Him, follow His teachings, and trust in His guidance.

*How can you make sure you are listening to
Jesus and following His lead in your life?*

You shall set apart three cities for yourselves in the land that the
Lord your God is giving you to possess.
Deuteronomy 19:2

God instructed the Israelites to set aside cities of refuge where someone who accidentally killed another person could flee for safety. These cities provided protection until the accused could stand trial and ensured that justice was served fairly.

The cities of refuge symbolize God's provision of safety and mercy. In Christ, we find our ultimate refuge, a place of safety where we can find forgiveness and protection from the consequences of sin.

How can you seek refuge in God when you are facing challenges or difficulties?

A single witness shall not suffice against a person for any crime
or for any wrong in connection with any offense that he has
committed. Only on the evidence of two witnesses or of three
witnesses shall a charge be established.
Deuteronomy 19:15

God established a standard for justice among the Israelites, requiring the testimony of two or three witnesses to confirm a charge. This ensured that accusations were taken seriously but also protected individuals from false accusations.

Justice and truth are important to God. We should be careful not to make judgments based on insufficient evidence or rumors. Instead, we should seek the truth and ensure that justice is upheld.

How can you ensure that you are fair and just in your dealings with others?

Your eye shall not pity. It shall be life for life, eye for eye,
tooth for tooth, hand for hand, foot for foot.
Deuteronomy 19:21

This principle, known as "Lex Talionis," ensured that justice was fair and proportionate. It was meant to prevent excessive punishment and to maintain balance in the legal system. The idea was that the punishment should fit the crime, neither too lenient nor too harsh.

Jesus later taught us a higher principle of mercy and forgiveness, encouraging us to turn the other cheek and go beyond just fairness to show love and grace. Justice is important, but so is mercy.

How can you balance justice and mercy in your
own life when dealing with others?

When you go out to war against your enemies and see horses and
chariots and an army larger than your own, you shall not be
afraid of them, for the Lord your God is with you, who brought
you up out of the land of Egypt.
Deuteronomy 20:1

God reassured the Israelites that they did not need to fear their enemies, no matter how powerful they appeared. The reminder of God's past deliverance from Egypt was meant to strengthen their faith and courage as they faced new challenges.

We all face battles in life, but God's presence with us means we never have to fight alone. He is our strength and our defender, just as He was for the Israelites.

What battles are you facing right now, and how
can you trust God to help you overcome them?

When you besiege a city for a long time, making war against it in order to take it, you shall not destroy its trees by wielding an axe against them. You may eat from them, but you shall not cut them down. Are the trees in the field human, that they should be besieged by you?
Deuteronomy 20:19

Even in war, God commanded the Israelites to protect fruit-bearing trees, emphasizing the importance of preserving resources and respecting creation. The trees were a source of food and should not be destroyed needlessly.

God cares about how we treat the world He created. We are called to be good stewards of the environment, caring for it responsibly and preserving it for future generations.

How can you take care of the environment and the resources God has given us?

And the elders of that city shall take the man and whip him, and
they shall fine him a hundred shekels of silver and give them to
the father of the young woman, because he has brought a bad
name upon a virgin of Israel. And she shall be his wife.
He may not divorce her all his days.
Deuteronomy 22:18–19

Elders in the community had the responsibility of ensuring justice and protecting the reputation of individuals, particularly in matters of marriage. Their role was crucial in maintaining the social and moral order of the community.

Leaders and elders today also have a responsibility to uphold justice and protect the integrity of the community. We are called to respect and support those in positions of authority who seek to do what is right.

How can you support the leaders and elders in your community or church?

You shall not see your brothers' ox or his sheep going astray and
ignore them. You shall take them back to your brother.
Deuteronomy 22:1

God instructed the Israelites to return lost property to its rightful owner, emphasizing the importance of responsibility and care for others' belongings. This law promoted community and trust among God's people.

Being responsible and caring for others' possessions is a reflection of our love for them. It's important to act with integrity and ensure that we are helping others rather than taking advantage of situations.

Have you ever found something that didn't belong to you?
What did you do with it?

If you make a vow to the Lord your God, you shall not delay
fulfilling it, for the Lord your God will surely require it of you,
and you will be guilty of sin.
Deuteronomy 23:21

When the Israelites made vows to God, they were expected to keep them without delay. This teaches us the importance of integrity and being true to our word, especially when making commitments to God and others.

God values honesty and faithfulness. When we make promises, whether to God or others, we should follow through and fulfill them. This builds trust and shows our respect for those around us.

Have you made any promises or commitments that you need to fulfill?

You shall not charge interest on loans to your brother, interest on
money, interest on food, interest on anything that is lent for interest.
Deuteronomy 23:19

God commanded the Israelites not to charge interest on loans to their fellow Israelites, encouraging them to help each other without expecting something in return. This law fostered a sense of community and support among God's people.

We are called to help those in need without expecting to gain from it. True generosity comes from a heart that gives freely, just as God freely gives to us.

How can you help someone in need without expecting anything in return?

You shall not oppress a hired worker who is poor and needy,
whether he is one of your brothers or one of the sojourners
who are in your land within your towns.
Deuteronomy 24:14

God commanded the Israelites to treat hired workers fairly, especially those who were poor and needy. This law reminded them of their responsibility to care for the vulnerable and to ensure justice for everyone.

God's heart is for the poor and the vulnerable, and He calls us to treat them with kindness and fairness. We should look out for those who are in need and do what we can to support them.

How can you show kindness to someone who might be vulnerable or in need?

*You shall remember that you were a slave in the land of Egypt;
therefore I command you to do this.*
Deuteronomy 24:18

God often reminded the Israelites of their past as slaves in Egypt, urging them to remember His deliverance and to act justly toward others. This remembrance was meant to keep them humble and compassionate, knowing that God had rescued them.

We, too, need to remember where God has brought us from and how He has delivered us. This helps us stay grateful and motivates us to show compassion to others who might be struggling.

What has God delivered you from, and how can you help others who are going through similar struggles?

*When you reap your harvest in your field and forget a sheaf in the
field, you shall not go back to get it. It shall be for the sojourner,
the fatherless, and the widow, that the Lord your
God may bless you in all the work of your hands.*
Deuteronomy 24:19

God instructed the Israelites to leave behind some of their harvests for the poor, the fatherless, and the widows. This law encouraged generosity and care for the less fortunate, trusting that God would bless their obedience.

We can learn from this to be generous with what we have, not hoarding everything for ourselves but sharing with those who are in need. God blesses us when we are generous and thoughtful of others.

How can you share what you have with someone who needs it today?

If brothers dwell together, and one of them dies and has no son,
the wife of the dead man shall not be married outside the family
to a stranger. Her husband's brother shall go in to her and take her
as his wife and perform the duty of a husband's brother to her.
Deuteronomy 25:5

In ancient Israel, keeping a family's name alive was incredibly important. If a man died without a son, his brother was expected to marry the widow and have children to carry on the family name. This law emphasized the value of family and the responsibility to care for one another.

While this specific practice isn't common today, the principle of caring for family and honoring commitments remains relevant. We are called to support our families and ensure that we do our part to uphold family bonds.

How can you show commitment and care to your family members?

You shall not have in your bag two kinds of weights,
a large and a small. You shall not have in your house
two kinds of measures, a large and a small.
Deuteronomy 25:13–14

God instructed the Israelites to be honest in their business dealings, using accurate weights and measures. This law promoted fairness and integrity, ensuring that no one was cheated or taken advantage of.

Integrity in all areas of life, including business, is crucial. God sees how we conduct ourselves, and He desires that we be fair and just in all our dealings.

Is there an area in your life where you need
to practice more honesty and fairness?

Remember what Amalek did to you on the way as you came out of Egypt.
Deuteronomy 25:17

The Amalekites attacked the Israelites when they were vulnerable, just after leaving Egypt. God commanded the Israelites to remember this act of treachery and to deal with the Amalekites accordingly. This remembrance was meant to keep them vigilant against future threats.

While we may not face literal enemies like the Amalekites, we are reminded to stay alert to spiritual dangers and to remember the lessons from our past. God calls us to be wise and to learn from our experiences.

What past experiences have taught you valuable lessons that you should remember?

You shall take some of the first of all the fruit of the ground, which
you harvest from your land that the Lord your God is giving you,
and you shall put it in a basket, and you shall go to the place that
the Lord your God will choose, to make his name dwell there.
Deuteronomy 26:2

God instructed the Israelites to bring the first fruits of their harvest to the place of worship, offering them to God in gratitude for His provision. This act of giving the first and best to God was a way of acknowledging His blessings and trusting Him for future provision.

We, too, are called to give God our first and best, whether it's our time, talents, or resources. Offering our first fruits is a way of showing our gratitude and dependence on God.

How can you offer the first fruits of your life to God?

And the Lord has declared today that you are a people for his treasured possession, as he has promised you, and that you are to keep all his commandments, and that he will set you in praise and in fame and in honor high above all nations that he has made, and that you shall be a people holy to the Lord your God, as he promised.
Deuteronomy 26:18-19

God reminded the Israelites that they were His treasured possession, set apart to be holy and to follow His commandments. This identity as a holy people came with the responsibility to live according to God's standards and to be a light to the nations.

As followers of Christ, we are also called to be holy and to live in a way that reflects God's character. Our lives should show others what it means to belong to God.

What does it mean to you to be part of God's holy people?

And on the day you cross over the Jordan to the land that the Lord your God is giving you, you shall set up large stones and plaster them with plaster. And you shall write on them all the words of this law, when you cross over to enter the land that the Lord your God is giving you, a land flowing with milk and honey, as the Lord, the God of your fathers, has promised you.
Deuteronomy 27:2-3

God commanded the Israelites to set up stones and write His law on them when they crossed the Jordan River into the Promised Land. This act served as a powerful reminder of God's word and His promises as they entered a new chapter in their journey.

In our lives, it's important to set up reminders of God's word and His faithfulness. These can be physical reminders like Bible verses on the wall or simply making a habit of recalling God's promises.

How can you set up reminders of God's word in your daily life?

*And if you faithfully obey the voice of the Lord your God, being
careful to do all his commandments that I command you today,
the Lord your God will set you high above all the nations of the
earth. And all these blessings shall come upon you and overtake
you, if you obey the voice of the Lord your God.*
Deuteronomy 28:1-2

God promised the Israelites that if they obeyed His commands, they
would receive abundant blessings. These blessings were a direct result of their
faithfulness and dedication to God's ways.

Obedience to God brings blessings into our lives. When we follow His
guidance, we experience His favor, protection, and provision. It's not always
easy, but the rewards of living in obedience to God are worth it.

What are some ways you can practice obedience to God today?

DAY 258: CURSES FOR DISOBEDIENCE

*But if you will not obey the voice of the Lord your God or be careful to
do all his commandments and his statutes that I command you today,
then all these curses shall come upon you and overtake you.*
Deuteronomy 28:15

Just as there were blessings for obedience, there were also curses for disobedience. God warned the Israelites that turning away from His commandments would lead to negative consequences, affecting every area of their lives.

Disobedience to God's commands can bring difficulties and challenges
into our lives. It's a reminder that God's laws are meant to protect and guide
us, and turning away from them can lead to harm.

Are there any areas in your life where you need to turn back to God's ways?

*I call heaven and earth to witness against you today, that I have
set before you life and death, blessing and curse. Therefore choose
life, that you and your offspring may live.*
Deuteronomy 30:19

God gave the Israelites a choice between life and death, blessings and curses. He urged them to choose life by loving and obeying Him so that they and their descendants might live and thrive in the land He was giving them.

We face choices every day that can lead us toward life or death, spiritually speaking. Choosing life means following God's path, embracing His love, and living according to His word.

What choices can you make today to choose life and follow God?

*The Lord your God himself will go over before you. He will
destroy these nations before you, so that you shall dispossess them,
and Joshua will go over at your head, as the Lord has spoken.*
Deuteronomy 31:3

As the Israelites prepared to enter the Promised Land, God reassured them of His faithfulness. He promised to go before them and lead them to victory, just as He had done in the past. Joshua was appointed to lead them, but it was ultimately God who would ensure their success.

God's faithfulness is a constant in our lives. He goes before us, guiding our steps and ensuring that His promises are fulfilled. We can trust Him to lead us through every challenge.

How have you seen God's faithfulness in your life?

*Be strong and courageous, for you shall go with this people into
the land that the Lord has sworn to their fathers to give them,
and you shall put them in possession of it.*
Deuteronomy 31:7

Moses encouraged Joshua to be strong and courageous as he led the Israelites into the Promised Land. This command was not just about physical strength but also about having the courage to trust God and lead His people in obedience.

We all face situations that require strength and courage. Whether it's standing up for what's right or stepping out in faith, God calls us to be strong and courageous, knowing that He is with us every step of the way.

What situation in your life requires you to be strong and courageous?

*It is the Lord who goes before you. He will be with you; he will
not leave you or forsake you. Do not fear or be dismayed.*
Deuteronomy 31:8

As Joshua prepared to lead the Israelites, God gave him a powerful promise: He would never leave or forsake him. This assurance was meant to give Joshua confidence as he faced the challenges ahead.

We, too, can hold on to this promise. No matter what we go through, God is always with us. He never abandons us, and we can trust Him to guide and support us through every difficulty.

*How does knowing that God will never leave
you to change the way you face challenges?*

*When Moses had finished writing the words of this law in a book
to the very end, Moses commanded the Levites who carried the
ark of the covenant of the Lord, 'Take this Book of the Law and
put it by the side of the ark of the covenant of the Lord your God,
that it may be there for a witness against you.'*
Deuteronomy 31:24–26

Moses wrote down all the words of God's law and placed them beside the ark of the covenant as a witness against the Israelites. This meant that the law would serve as a constant reminder of God's standards and their commitment to follow Him.

The Bible serves as our witness today. It reminds us of God's truth and guides us in how to live according to His will. Keeping God's word close is essential for staying on the right path.

How can you make God's word a more constant presence in your life?

*Then Moses spoke the words of this song until they were finished,
in the ears of all the assembly of Israel.*
Deuteronomy 31:30

Moses taught the Israelites a song that recounted God's faithfulness and the consequences of turning away from Him. This song was meant to be a reminder for future generations of the importance of staying true to God.

Songs can be powerful tools for remembering important truths. Just like the Israelites, we can use songs to remind us of God's goodness and to keep our hearts aligned with His will.

What songs help you remember God's faithfulness?

The Rock, his work is perfect, for all his ways are justice. A God of faithfulness and without iniquity, just and upright is he.
Deuteronomy 32:4

In Moses' song, he describes God as the Rock, whose work is perfect and whose ways are just. This imagery highlights God's unchanging nature and His absolute righteousness. No matter what happens, God remains a solid foundation on which we can stand.

Reflecting on God's greatness helps us trust Him more deeply. Knowing that He is perfect, just, and faithful gives us confidence to rely on Him in every situation.

How does understanding God's greatness impact your faith?

The Lord alone guided him, no foreign god was with him.
Deuteronomy 32:12

In the song of Moses, he recalls how God alone guided Israel, with no help from any foreign gods. This emphasizes God's exclusive role as the true guide and protector of His people. The Israelites were to remember that it was God alone who led them through the wilderness and into the Promised Land.

In our lives, it's important to recognize that God is our true guide. We should be careful not to put our trust in things or people that might lead us away from Him. God is faithful, and He will guide us if we trust Him.

What are some ways you can rely more on God's guidance in your life?

You were unmindful of the Rock that bore you,
and you forgot the God who gave you birth.
Deuteronomy 32:18

Moses warns the Israelites about the danger of forgetting God's goodness. Despite all that God had done for them, they tended to forget and turn away from Him. This forgetfulness led to disobedience and hardship.

We, too, can fall into the trap of forgetting God's goodness, especially when things are going well. It's important to regularly remind ourselves of how God has worked in our lives and to stay mindful of His ongoing presence and provision.

How can you remind yourself of God's goodness today?

For a fire is kindled by my anger, and it burns to the depths of
Sheol, devours the earth and its increase, and sets on fire the
foundations of the mountains.
Deuteronomy 32:22

Moses' song also speaks of the severe consequences of turning away from God. God's anger is described as a consuming fire that can bring destruction. This serves as a sobering reminder of the seriousness of disobedience.

Disobedience to God's commands has real consequences. While God is loving and merciful, He is also just, and He takes sin seriously. Understanding this helps us to strive to live in obedience to His word.

What areas of your life do you need to bring
into greater alignment with God's will?

*For the Lord will vindicate his people and have compassion on his servants,
when he sees that their power is gone and there is none remaining, bond or free.*
Deuteronomy 32:36

Despite the warnings of judgment, Moses also speaks of God's compassion. When God sees that His people are in need, He has mercy on them and comes to their aid. This shows that God's love and compassion are always available, even when we fall short.

God's compassion is a source of hope for us. No matter how far we stray, He is always ready to forgive and restore us when we turn back to Him. His love never fails.

How has God shown His compassion in your life?

*See now that I, even I, am he, and there is no god beside me; I kill and I make
alive; I wound and I heal; and there is none that can deliver out of my hand.*
Deuteronomy 32:39

God declares that there is no other god besides Him. He alone has the power over life and death, and no one can escape His hand. This is a powerful statement of God's sovereignty and the uniqueness of His divine nature.

Understanding that there is no god like our God gives us confidence and security. We can trust in His power, His justice, and His love, knowing that He is in control of all things.

What does it mean to you that God is sovereign over everything?

*Vengeance is mine, and recompense, for the time when their foot shall slip;
for the day of their calamity is at hand, and their doom comes swiftly.*
Deuteronomy 32:35

God reminds the Israelites that vengeance belongs to Him alone. He will repay those who do wrong at the right time. This verse teaches that we should leave justice in God's hands rather than seeking revenge ourselves.

When others wrong us, it can be tempting to take matters into our own hands. However, God calls us to trust Him to make things right. He sees everything, and He will bring justice in His perfect timing.

How can you trust God to handle situations where you've been wronged?

*Rejoice with him, O heavens; bow down to him, all gods, for he avenges
the blood of his children and takes vengeance on his adversaries. He
repays those who hate him and cleanses his people's land.*
Deuteronomy 32:43

In this verse, Moses speaks of God's ultimate victory over His enemies and His provision of atonement for His people. God not only defends His children but also purifies and cleanses them from sin.

God's provision of atonement is a powerful reminder of His love and mercy. Through Jesus, we have received the ultimate atonement for our sins, allowing us to be cleansed and restored to a right relationship with God.

What does it mean to you that God has provided atonement for your sins?

*This is the blessing with which Moses the man of God blessed the
people of Israel before his death.*
Deuteronomy 33:1

As Moses' time on earth was coming to an end, he blessed the people
of Israel. This final blessing was a way for Moses to pass on God's favor and
promises to the next generation as they prepared to enter the Promised Land.

Blessing others is an important part of our faith. We can speak words of
life and encouragement to those around us, just as Moses did. These blessings
can have a lasting impact on others' lives.

How can you bless someone today?

*There is none like God, O Jeshurun, who rides through the
heavens to your help, through the skies in his majesty.*
Deuteronomy 33:26

Moses reminds the Israelites that there is no one like their God. He is
powerful and majestic, riding through the heavens to help His people. This
image of God as a mighty helper is meant to inspire confidence and trust.

We all face situations where we need help beyond what we can provide
ourselves. God is always ready to come to our aid with His great power and
strength. We can rely on Him in every circumstance.

What situation in your life do you need God's help with right now?

The eternal God is your dwelling place,
and underneath are the everlasting arms.
Deuteronomy 33:27

In Moses' blessing, he describes God as the eternal dwelling place for His people and speaks of God's everlasting arms supporting them. This imagery conveys the idea of God's constant protection and care.

No matter what we go through, we are held securely in God's everlasting arms. He is our refuge, our strength, and our safety. We can find peace in knowing that He is always there to support us.

How does knowing that you are held in God's everlasting arms give you peace?

So Moses the servant of the Lord died there in the land of Moab,
according to the word of the Lord.
Deuteronomy 34:5

Moses, the great leader who brought the Israelites out of Egypt and guided them through the wilderness, has passed away. Though he was not permitted to enter the Promised Land, God allowed him to see it from Mount Nebo. His death marked the end of an era, but his legacy lived on through the people he led.

Moses' life reminds us that while our time on earth is finite, the impact we make can endure. Like Moses, we are called to faithfully serve God and trust Him with the outcome of our work.

How can you create a lasting impact through your service to God and others?

DAY 277: JOSHUA TAKES LEADERSHIP

*And Joshua the son of Nun was full of the spirit of wisdom, for
Moses had laid his hands on him. So the people of Israel obeyed
him and did as the Lord had commanded Moses.*
Deuteronomy 34:9

With Moses' death, Joshua stepped into his new role as the leader of Israel. Filled with the spirit of wisdom, Joshua was well-prepared to guide the Israelites into the Promised Land. The people recognized his leadership and followed him just as they had followed Moses.

Joshua's transition into leadership teaches us the importance of preparing the next generation. By mentoring others and passing on what we've learned, we ensure that God's work continues.

Who can you mentor or guide to help them grow in their faith and leadership?

DAY 278: BE STRONG AND COURAGEOUS

*Have I not commanded you? Be strong and courageous.
Do not be frightened, and do not be dismayed, for the
Lord your God is with you wherever you go.*
Joshua 1:9

As Joshua prepared to lead the Israelites into the Promised Land, God gave him this powerful command: to be strong and courageous. God reassured Joshua that He would be with him every step of the way, giving him the strength and courage needed to face any challenge.

In our lives, we often face daunting tasks or uncertain futures. But like Joshua, we can find strength and courage in the knowledge that God is always with us, guiding and supporting us.

*What situation in your life requires you to be strong
and courageous, trusting in God's presence?*

*And Joshua commanded the officers of the people, 'Pass through the
midst of the camp and command the people, "Prepare your provisions,
for within three days you are to pass over this Jordan to go in to take
possession of the land that the Lord your God is giving you to possess.*
Joshua 1:10–11

The time had come for the Israelites to finally enter the Promised Land.
Joshua instructed the people to prepare themselves, for in three days, they
would cross the Jordan River and take possession of the land God had promised them. This was a moment of great anticipation and faith.

Crossing the Jordan symbolizes stepping into God's promises. It often requires preparation, faith, and the willingness to move forward even when the
path is uncertain.

*What steps of faith do you need to take to move
forward into what God has promised you?*

*And Joshua the son of Nun sent two men secretly from Shittim
as spies, saying, 'Go, view the land, especially Jericho.' And they
went and came into the house of a prostitute whose name was
Rahab and lodged there.*
Joshua 2:1

Before taking Jericho, Joshua sent two spies to gather information. They
found refuge in the house of Rahab, a woman of unexpected faith. Rahab recognized the power of the God of Israel and chose to protect the spies, securing
her and her family's safety in the process.

Rahab's story is a powerful reminder that faith can be found in unexpected places and people. God often works through those we might least expect,
showing His grace and mercy.

How can you be open to seeing God's work in unexpected places or people?

*So when the people set out from their tents to pass over the Jordan
with the priests bearing the ark of the covenant before the people,
… the waters coming down from above stood and rose up in a
heap very far away.*
Joshua 3:14-16

As the Israelites prepared to cross the Jordan River, the priests carrying the Ark of the Covenant stepped into the water, and immediately the river stopped flowing. The waters rose up in a heap, allowing the people to cross on dry ground, just as their ancestors had crossed the Red Sea. This miraculous event signified God's continued presence and faithfulness as they entered the Promised Land.

Crossing the Jordan was a defining moment for the Israelites, a testament to God's power and their obedience. It reminds us that when we step out in faith, God will make a way, even when the path seems impossible.

*What "Jordan" in your life is God calling you to cross,
trusting that He will make a way?*

*When all the nation had finished passing over the Jordan, the Lord said to
Joshua, 'Take twelve men from the people, from each tribe a man, and command
them, saying, "Take twelve stones from here out of the midst of the Jordan, from
the very place where the priests' feet stood firmly, and bring them over with you
and lay them down in the place where you lodge tonight.*
Joshua 4:1-3

After the Israelites crossed the Jordan River, God instructed Joshua to have twelve men, one from each tribe, take a stone from the riverbed. These stones were to be set up as a memorial, a reminder to future generations of how God had miraculously brought them into the Promised Land.

Memorials like these help us remember God's faithfulness. They serve as tangible reminders of His power and provision in our lives, encouraging us and future generations to trust in Him.

What are the memorials in your life that remind you of God's faithfulness?

On that day the Lord exalted Joshua in the sight of all Israel, and
they stood in awe of him, just as they had stood in awe of Moses,
all the days of his life.
Joshua 4:14

As the Israelites crossed the Jordan, God exalted Joshua in the eyes of the people. Just as they had revered Moses, they now stood in awe of Joshua, recognizing that God's hand was upon him. This was a significant moment of leadership transition, affirming Joshua's role as the new leader of Israel.

God exalts those who humbly follow His will. Joshua's leadership was not about his strength but about his obedience to God. When we faithfully follow God, He lifts us in His time and for His purposes.

How can you humbly follow God's will, trusting Him to lift you in His time?

DAY 284: GILGAL, THE PLACE OF RENEWAL

The people came up out of the Jordan on the tenth day of the first month,
and they encamped at Gilgal on the east border of Jericho. And those
twelve stones, which they took out of the Jordan, Joshua set up at Gilgal.
Joshua 4:19-20

After crossing the Jordan, the Israelites camped at Gilgal, where Joshua set up the twelve stones as a memorial. Gilgal became a place of renewal for the Israelites, where they reaffirmed their covenant with God before moving forward to conquer the land.

Gilgal represents those moments in our lives where we pause, reflect, and renew our commitment to God. It's essential to take time to remember God's faithfulness and to prepare ourselves for the next steps in our journey with Him.

Where is your "Gilgal" - a place or moment where
you can renew your commitment to God?

At that time the Lord said to Joshua, 'Make flint knives and
circumcise the sons of Israel a second time.
Joshua 5:2

Before the Israelites could proceed to conquer the Promised Land, God instructed Joshua to circumcise the men of Israel. This act was a physical sign of the covenant between God and His people, reminding them of their identity and commitment to Him.

Circumcision was a necessary step of obedience for the Israelites before they could enter fully into the promises of God. Likewise, God often calls us to acts of obedience that reaffirm our identity in Him before we move forward in His plans.

What steps of obedience is God calling you to take
as a sign of your commitment to Him?

And the day after the Passover, on that very day, they ate of the
produce of the land, unleavened cakes and parched grain. And the
manna ceased the day after they ate of the produce of the land, and
there was no longer manna for the people of Israel, but they ate of
the fruit of the land of Canaan that year.
Joshua 5:11-12

For forty years, God had provided manna from heaven to sustain the Israelites in the wilderness. But now, as they entered the Promised Land and began to eat its produce, the manna ceased. This marked the beginning of a new chapter in their journey, where they would rely on the fruit of the land that God had given them.

God's provision changes as we move through different seasons of life. He provides exactly what we need for each stage of our journey. As we enter new phases, we can trust that God will continue to provide, even if it looks different than before.

How has God's provision changed in your life
as you've moved through different seasons?

When Joshua was by Jericho, he lifted up his eyes and looked, and behold, a man was standing before him with his drawn sword in his hand. And Joshua went to him and said to him, 'Are you for us, or for our adversaries?' And he said, 'No; but I am the commander of the army of the Lord. Now I have come.'
Joshua 5:13-14

As Joshua approached Jericho, he encountered a mysterious figure with a drawn sword – the commander of the Lord's army. This encounter reminded Joshua that the battles ahead would not be fought in his strength but with the power of God's heavenly armies.

We often face challenges that seem insurmountable. But like Joshua, we need to recognize that we are not alone. God fights for us, and His power is far greater than any obstacle we face.

In what areas of your life do you need to trust that God is fighting for you?

And the Lord said to Joshua, 'See, I have given Jericho into your hand, with its king and mighty men of valor. You shall march around the city, all the men of war going around the city once. Thus shall you do for six days.'
Joshua 6:2-3

God gave Joshua specific instructions for conquering Jericho. Rather than attacking directly, the Israelites were to march around the city for six days, and on the seventh day, they were to march around seven times, blowing trumpets and shouting. When they obeyed, the walls of Jericho fell, and the city was theirs.

Jericho's fall teaches us that God's methods often defy human logic. When we follow His instructions, even when they seem unconventional, He brings victory in ways we could never imagine.

How can you trust God's unconventional methods in your current challenges?

Joshua laid an oath on them at that time, saying, 'Cursed before
the Lord be the man who rises up and rebuilds this city, Jericho.
At the cost of his firstborn shall he lay its foundation, and at the
cost of his youngest son shall he set up its gates.'
Joshua 6:26

After the victory at Jericho, Joshua declared a curse on anyone who would attempt to rebuild the city. Jericho was not to be restored as a symbol of God's judgment and victory. This curse was a reminder of the seriousness of disobedience to God's commands.

There are things in our lives that God has torn down for a reason. We must be careful not to rebuild what God has destroyed, whether it be old habits, toxic relationships, or sinful behaviors.

Is there something in your life that God has torn
down that you need to let go of for good?

DAY 290: THE SIN OF ACHAN

But the people of Israel broke faith in regard to the devoted things,
for Achan the son of Carmi… took some of the devoted things.
And the anger of the Lord burned against the people of Israel.
Joshua 7:1

Despite the clear instructions to destroy everything in Jericho, Achan disobeyed and kept some of the devoted items for himself. His sin brought God's judgment not only on himself but on the entire community, leading to a devastating defeat at the next battle.

Achan's sin reminds us of the serious consequences of disobedience and hidden sin. Our actions, whether good or bad, can impact more than just ourselves—they can affect those around us as well.

Is there any hidden sin in your life that you
need to confess and bring into the light?

So about three thousand men went up there from the people. And they fled before the men of Ai, and the men of Ai killed about thirty-six of their men and chased them before the gate as far as Shebarim and struck them at the descent. And the hearts of the people melted and became as water.
Joshua 7:4-5

The Israelites, confident after their victory at Jericho, underestimated the town of Ai and were defeated. This defeat was a direct result of Achan's sin, which had brought God's disfavor upon the entire nation. It served as a humbling reminder that victory only comes through obedience to God.

Defeat can be a powerful teacher. It reminds us to rely on God's strength rather than our own and to ensure that we are walking in obedience to His commands.

What lessons can you learn from times of defeat or failure in your life?

And Joshua said to Achan, 'My son, give glory to the Lord God of Israel and give praise to him. And tell me now what you have done; do not hide it from me.' And Achan answered Joshua, 'Truly I have sinned against the Lord God of Israel, and this is what I did … then I coveted them and took them.'
Joshua 7:19-21

When confronted by Joshua, Achan confessed his sin. He had taken what was devoted to destruction and hidden it in his tent. Achan's sin was exposed, and it had devastating consequences—not just for him but for his family and the entire nation.

Sin, when hidden, festers and brings destruction. But when we confess and bring it into the light, we can begin the process of healing and restoration. God calls us to live transparently, confessing our sins to Him and to one another.

Is there something you need to confess today to bring into the light before God and others?

*And Joshua and all Israel with him took Achan the son of Zerah,
and the silver, and the cloak, and the bar of gold, and his sons and
daughters, and his oxen and donkeys and sheep, and his tent and
all that he had. And they brought them up to the Valley of Achor.
And Joshua said, 'Why did you bring trouble on us? The Lord brings
trouble on you today.' And all Israel stoned him with stones.*
Joshua 7:24-25

Achan's sin brought him and his family to the Valley of Achor, which
means the "Valley of Trouble." There, he faced the consequences of his actions.
The punishment was severe, but it was necessary to cleanse the community and
restore God's favor.

The Valley of Achor reminds us that sin brings trouble and that there are
consequences for our actions. But it also points to God's desire for holiness
among His people and the need to take sin seriously.

Are there areas in your life where you need to take sin more seriously?

*And the Lord said to Joshua, 'Do not fear and do not be dismayed. Take
all the fighting men with you, and arise, go up to Ai. See, I have given
into your hand the king of Ai, and his people, his city, and his land.'*
Joshua 8:1

After dealing with Achan's sin, God renewed His promise to Joshua. This
time, when Israel went up against Ai, they followed God's instructions carefully and won a decisive victory. The defeat of Ai was a reminder that victory
comes through obedience to God.

God is a God of second chances. When we repent and return to Him, He
renews His promises to us and leads us to victory. No matter how far we've
fallen, there is always a way back to God's grace

How can you return to God and trust Him for victory in your life?

At that time Joshua built an altar to the Lord, the God of Israel, on Mount Ebal, just as Moses the servant of the Lord had commanded the people of Israel… And there, in the presence of the people of Israel, he wrote on the stones a copy of the law of Moses, which he had written.
Joshua 8:30-32

After their victory at Ai, Joshua led the Israelites to Mount Ebal, where he built an altar to the Lord. There, he wrote the law of Moses on the stones and read it aloud to the people. This was a moment of renewal, where the people recommitted themselves to the covenant with God.

Building an altar is a way of marking significant spiritual milestones in our lives. It's a time to pause, reflect, and renew our commitment to God's Word and His ways.

What "altar" can you build in your life to mark a moment of spiritual renewal?

But when the inhabitants of Gibeon heard what Joshua had done to Jericho and to Ai, they on their part acted with cunning… and they went to Joshua in the camp at Gilgal and said to him and to the men of Israel, 'We have come from a distant country, so now make a covenant with us.'
Joshua 9:3-6

The Gibeonites, fearing Israel's advance, resorted to deception. They dressed in worn-out clothes and carried moldy bread, pretending to be from a distant land. Without seeking the Lord's counsel, Joshua and the Israelites made a covenant with them, only to discover later that the Gibeonites were their neighbors.

This story warns us of the dangers of making decisions without seeking God's guidance. Even when things seem clear or harmless, we must always consult God in prayer and seek His wisdom.

Are there decisions in your life where you need to seek God's counsel before moving forward?

*Then all the leaders said to all the congregation, 'We have sworn
to them by the Lord, the God of Israel, and now we may not touch
them. This we will do to them: let them live, lest wrath be upon
us, because of the oath that we swore to them.'*
Joshua 9:19–20

Even though the Gibeonites had deceived them, the Israelites honored the covenant they had made. They recognized the importance of keeping their word, especially since they had sworn the oath in the name of the Lord. The Gibeonites were allowed to live, but they became servants to the Israelites.

This teaches us the importance of integrity and honoring our commitments, even when it's difficult. God expects us to keep our word and to act with integrity in all our dealings.

How can you demonstrate integrity in your commitments and promises today?

*Then Joshua spoke to the Lord in the day when the Lord gave
the Amorites over to the sons of Israel, and he said in the sight
of Israel, 'Sun, stand still at Gibeon, and moon, in the Valley of
Aijalon.' And the sun stood still, and the moon stopped, until the
nation took vengeance on their enemies.*
Joshua 10:12–13

In one of the most extraordinary miracles recorded in the Bible, Joshua prayed for the sun to stand still so that the Israelites could finish their battle against the Amorites. God answered Joshua's prayer, and the sun did not set until the battle was won.

This event reminds us of God's power over creation and His willingness to intervene on behalf of His people. When we pray in faith, God can do the impossible.

*What impossible situation are you facing today
that you need to bring to God in prayer?*

*And Joshua captured all these kings and their land at one time,
because the Lord God of Israel fought for Israel.*
Joshua 10:42

After the battle at Gibeon, Joshua led the Israelites in a campaign against the southern cities of Canaan. One by one, they defeated the kings and captured their cities, all because the Lord fought for Israel. The Southern campaign was a clear demonstration of God's power and faithfulness.

When we face battles in life, it's important to remember that God fights for us. He is our strength and our shield, and with Him, we can overcome any obstacle.

How can you trust God to fight for you in the battles you are facing today?

DAY 300: THE NORTHERN CAMPAIGN

*So Joshua took all that land, the hill country and all the Negeb
and all the land of Goshen and the lowland and the Arabah and
the hill country of Israel and its lowland from Mount Halak,
which rises toward Seir, as far as Baal-gad in the Valley of
Lebanon below Mount Hermon. And he captured all their kings
and struck them and put them to death.*
Joshua 11:16-17

After the southern campaign, Joshua turned his attention to the northern kings of Canaan. With God's help, the Israelites conquered the northern territories, taking control of the entire land that God had promised them. This was the fulfillment of God's promise to Abraham, Isaac, and Jacob.

God's promises are sure. What He has spoken, He will bring to pass. We may not always see the fulfillment immediately, but we can trust that God is faithful to keep His word.

What promise from God are you holding onto today, trusting Him to fulfill?

So Joshua took the whole land, according to all that the Lord had spoken to Moses. And Joshua gave it for an inheritance to Israel according to their tribal allotments. And the land had rest from war.
Joshua 11:23

After years of battles and conquest, the Israelites finally took possession of the Promised Land, and the land had rest from war. This was a time of peace and fulfillment, as God's promises were realized and the people began to settle in their new homes.

Rest is an important part of our spiritual journey. After seasons of struggle and toil, God provides times of rest and renewal. These are moments to reflect on His goodness and to enjoy the fruits of His promises.

How can you find rest in God today, trusting in His provision and faithfulness?

Now therefore divide this land for an inheritance to the nine tribes and half the tribe of Manasseh.
Joshua 13:7

With the land conquered, it was time to divide it among the tribes of Israel. Joshua carefully distributed the land according to God's instructions, ensuring that each tribe received its inheritance. This division of the land was a fulfillment of God's promise and a sign of His provision.

God has a specific inheritance for each of us. He knows what we need and has prepared a place for us in His kingdom. Our task is to trust Him and to receive what He has allotted for us with gratitude and faith.

What inheritance has God prepared for you,
and how can you receive it with gratitude?

Then the people of Judah came to Joshua at Gilgal. And Caleb the son of Jephunneh the Kenizzite said to him, 'You know what the Lord said to Moses the man of God in Kadesh-barnea concerning you and me. I was forty years old when Moses the servant of the Lord sent me from Kadesh-barnea to spy out the land, and I brought him word again as it was in my heart.'
Joshua 14:6-7

Caleb, one of the original spies sent into Canaan, was now 85 years old. Yet, his faith in God had not wavered. He reminded Joshua of the promise God had made to him and boldly asked for his inheritance: the hill country of Hebron. Caleb's faith and perseverance were rewarded as he received his promised land.

Caleb's story is an inspiration to remain steadfast in our faith, no matter how much time has passed. God's promises are worth waiting for, and He rewards those who remain faithful.

What promise from God are you holding onto, and how can you continue to trust Him for its fulfillment?

Then the Lord said to Joshua, 'Say to the people of Israel, "Appoint the cities of refuge, of which I spoke to you through Moses, that the manslayer who kills any person without intent or unknowingly may flee there. They shall be for you a refuge from the avenger of blood."
Joshua 20:1-3

God instructed Joshua to designate cities of refuge—safe havens for those who accidentally caused the death of another person. These cities were places where people could flee to avoid revenge and ensure a fair trial. The cities of refuge illustrate God's mercy and justice, providing protection and fairness to those in need.

In Christ, we find our ultimate refuge. When we sin or face accusations, we can run to Him for mercy, forgiveness, and protection. He is our safe place, where we find grace and shelter from the storms of life.

How can you seek refuge in Christ today, finding peace and protection in His presence?

Then the heads of the fathers' houses of the Levites came to Eleazar the priest and to Joshua the son of Nun and to the heads of the fathers' houses of the tribes of the people of Israel. And they said to them at Shiloh in the land of Canaan, 'The Lord commanded through Moses that we be given cities to dwell in, along with their pasturelands for our livestock.'
Joshua 21:1–2

Unlike the other tribes, the Levites did not receive a large portion of land. Instead, they were given cities scattered throughout Israel, along with pasturelands for their livestock. The Levites' inheritance was unique because their primary inheritance was the Lord Himself. They were called to serve Him in the temple and to minister to the people.

The Levites remind us that our true inheritance is not in worldly possessions but in our relationship with God. He is our portion, and in Him, we find everything we need.

How can you focus on your inheritance in God today, rather than on worldly possessions?

Thus the Lord gave to Israel all the land that he swore to give to their fathers. And they took possession of it, and they settled there. And the Lord gave them rest on every side just as he had sworn to their fathers. Not one of all their enemies had withstood them, for the Lord had given all their enemies into their hands.
Joshua 21:43–44

God fulfilled His promises to Israel. They received the land, took possession of it, and settled there. The Lord gave them rest on every side, just as He had sworn to their ancestors. Every promise was kept, and the people experienced peace and fulfillment in the land.

God is faithful to His promises. When we trust Him and follow His lead, He brings us to a place of rest and fulfillment. His word never fails, and His plans for us are good.

How can you rest in the fulfillment of God's promises today, trusting in His faithfulness?

*And Joshua said to all the people, 'Thus says the Lord, the God
of Israel, "Long ago, your fathers lived beyond the Euphrates, …
and they served other gods. Then I took your father Abraham from
beyond the River and led him through all the land of Canaan,
and made his offspring many. I gave him Isaac."*
Joshua 24:2–3

As Joshua neared the end of his life, he gathered the people and reminded them of God's faithfulness throughout their history. He recounted how God had chosen Abraham, led the Israelites out of Egypt, and brought them into the Promised Land. Joshua's farewell address was a call to remember God's goodness and to remain faithful to Him.

Reflecting on God's faithfulness in the past gives us confidence for the future. When we remember what God has done, we are encouraged to continue trusting Him and living in obedience to His word.

How can you remember and celebrate God's faithfulness in your life today?

*Now therefore fear the Lord and serve him in sincerity and in faithfulness. Put away
the gods that your fathers served beyond the River and in Egypt, and serve the Lord.
And if it is evil in your eyes to serve the Lord, choose this day whom you will serve,
whether the gods your fathers served in the region beyond the River, or the gods of the
Amorites in whose land you dwell. But as for me and my house, we will serve the Lord.*
Joshua 24:14–15

Joshua challenged the people to make a choice: would they serve the Lord, or would they follow the false gods of their ancestors and the surrounding nations? Joshua set the example by declaring that he and his household would serve the Lord.

Every day, we face the same choice. We can serve God with our whole heart, or we can be distracted by the idols of our time—whether they are money, success, or anything else that takes God's place in our lives.

What will you choose today–will you serve the Lord with all your heart?

And the people said to Joshua, 'The Lord our God we will serve, and his voice we will obey.' So Joshua made a covenant with the people that day and put in place statutes and rules for them at Shechem.
Joshua 24:24-25

The people responded to Joshua's challenge by renewing their covenant with God. They promised to serve the Lord and to obey His voice. Joshua then set up a large stone as a witness to their commitment, reminding them of the covenant they had made.

Renewing our commitment to God is essential. It's easy to drift away or to lose focus, but when we take time to renew our covenant with God, we are reminded of our purpose and calling.

How can you renew your commitment to God today, serving Him with renewed passion and obedience?

DAY 310: JOSHUA'S PASSING

After these things Joshua the son of Nun, the servant of the Lord, died, being 110 years old. And they buried him in his own inheritance at Timnath-serah, which is in the hill country of Ephraim, north of the mountain of Gaash.
Joshua 24:29-30

Joshua, the faithful leader of Israel, passed away at the age of 110. He was buried in the land he had helped conquer, in his inheritance in the hill country of Ephraim. Joshua's life was marked by faithfulness to God, courage, and obedience. His legacy was one of leading God's people into the Promised Land.

Joshua's life challenges us to live faithfully and courageously, following God's lead and trusting Him with the outcomes. Our time on earth is limited, but we can leave a lasting legacy by living for God's purposes.

How can you live today in a way that leaves a legacy of faithfulness and obedience to God?

*Eleazar son of Aaron died and was buried at Gibeah, the town
of his son Phinehas, which had been allotted to him in the hill
country of Ephraim.*
Joshua 24:33

Just like the end of a road trip when the car finally pulls into the driveway, we reach the close of an era in the story of Israel's journey to the Promised Land. Eleazar, the son of Aaron, served faithfully as a high priest, guiding the people in worship and ensuring they followed God's commands. His death marks the end of the generation that led Israel into their new home, just as the road trip ends and the travelers settle back into their familiar routines.

Eleazar's life reminds us that even the longest journeys eventually reach their end. Our journey through life is filled with moments of service, faithfulness, and dedication. And like Eleazar, when our journey ends, the legacy we leave behind is one of faithfulness to God's calling.

*How can you serve faithfully today, knowing that
your journey has a purpose and a destination?*

*The Israelites served the Lord throughout the lifetime of Joshua
and of the elders who outlived him and who had experienced
everything the Lord had done for Israel.*
Judges 2:7

After a long journey, it's natural to reflect on where we've been. The Israelites did the same after settling into the Promised Land. They remembered all that God had done for them, from their deliverance from Egypt to their victories in Canaan. It was a time of looking back and recognizing God's faithfulness.

Just like looking through old photos from a family road trip, we should take time to reflect on our journey with God. Remembering His faithfulness in the past gives us confidence for the future.

What moments in your life can you look back on to see God's faithfulness?

After that whole generation had been gathered to their ancestors,
another generation grew up who knew neither the Lord nor what
he had done for Israel.
Judges 2:10

As one journey ends, another begins. A new generation of Israelites grew up in the Promised Land, but they did not remember all that God had done. They hadn't experienced the miracles or seen God's power firsthand. This new generation struggled to follow the path that had been laid out for them.

It's important to share our stories with those who come after us. Just like telling stories from a road trip helps others understand the journey, sharing our experiences with God helps the next generation know Him better.

How can you share your journey with God to help others on their road?

Then the Israelites did evil in the eyes of the Lord and served the
Baals. They forsook the Lord, the God of their ancestors, who had
brought them out of Egypt.
Judges 2:11–12

The new generation of Israelites struggled to stay on the path God had set for them. Without firsthand experience of God's miracles, they began to stray. They turned to other gods, forgetting the one true God who had delivered them.

This part of the journey is like getting lost on a road trip. You take a wrong turn and end up somewhere you didn't intend to go. But even when we get lost, God is always ready to guide us back to the right path.

How can you stay focused on God's path today,
avoiding distractions that could lead you astray?

Then the Lord raised up judges,
who saved them out of the hands of these raiders.
Judges 2:16

Even when the Israelites strayed, God didn't abandon them. He raised up judges—leaders who would help guide the people back to Him and deliver them from their enemies. These judges were like signposts on a road trip, pointing the way back to the right path.

God is always merciful, ready to help us find our way back to Him when we get lost. No matter how far we stray, He is always near, ready to lead us home.

Where do you need God's guidance today to help you find your way back to Him?

Yet they would not listen to their judges but prostituted themselves to
other gods and worshiped them. They quickly turned from the ways of
their ancestors, who had been obedient to the Lord's commands.
Judges 2:17

Despite God's mercy and the leadership of the judges, the Israelites continued to turn away from God. Their disobedience led to difficult consequences—enemies overtook them, and their lives became filled with strife.

Disobedience on our journey with God can lead to unnecessary detours and hardships. But even when we make wrong choices, God remains patient and ready to guide us back.

What steps can you take today to ensure you're
following God's path rather than your own?

DAY 317: A CYCLE OF REBELLION AND RESCUE

Whenever the Lord raised up a judge for them, he was with the
judge and saved them out of the hands of their enemies as long
as the judge lived; for the Lord relented because of their groaning
under those who oppressed and afflicted them.
Judges 2:18

The story of the judges is a cycle of rebellion, consequences, and rescue. The Israelites would stray from God, face oppression, and cry out for help, and God would send a judge to rescue them. This cycle repeats itself throughout the book of Judges.

Our lives can sometimes feel like a cycle, too. We stray from God, face the consequences, and then cry out for help. But just as God was faithful to rescue the Israelites, He is faithful to rescue us, too.

Are there areas in your life where you need t
o break the cycle and fully return to God?

DAY 318: GIDEON'S CALL

The angel of the Lord appeared to Gideon, he said,
'The Lord is with you, mighty warrior.'
Judges 6:12

Gideon was an unlikely hero. He was hiding in a winepress when the angel of the Lord appeared to him and called him a mighty warrior. Gideon didn't see himself as a leader, but God did. God had a plan for Gideon, even if Gideon couldn't see it himself.

Sometimes, we don't feel up to the challenges ahead on our journey. But God sees us differently. He knows our potential and is with us every step of the way.

How can you trust God's calling in your life, even when you feel inadequate?

Gideon said to God, 'If you will save Israel by my hand as you have promised—look, I will place a wool fleece on the threshing floor.'
Judges 6:36–37

Gideon needed reassurance. He wasn't sure if God was calling him to lead Israel against their enemies, so he asked for a sign. He placed a fleece on the ground and asked God to make the fleece wet with dew while the ground stayed dry. God did as Gideon asked, confirming His promise.

Sometimes, we need reassurance on our journey. We want to be sure we're on the right path. God understands our need for assurance and is patient with our doubts.

What reassurance do you need from God today as you continue on your journey?

The Lord said to Gideon, 'You have too many men. I cannot deliver Midian into their hands, or Israel would boast against me, "My own strength has saved me."
Judges 7:2

Gideon had gathered a large army to fight the Midianites, but God told him he had too many men. God wanted to make sure that the Israelites knew their victory would come from Him, not from their strength. So, God reduced Gideon's army to just 300 men, and with those 300, God delivered Israel.

Our journey isn't about our strength; it's about trusting God. When we face overwhelming challenges, we can trust that God will fight for us and lead us to victory.

How can you trust God's strength in the battles you face today?

Gideon and the hundred men with him reached the edge of the camp at the beginning of the middle watch, just after they had changed the guard. They blew their trumpets and broke the jars that were in their hands.
Judges 7:19

Gideon obeyed God's instructions, even though they seemed unconventional. He and his men attacked the Midianite camp with trumpets and jars instead of swords. But their obedience led to victory as the Midianites were thrown into confusion and defeated each other.

Obedience to God's commands may sometimes seem strange or difficult, but it leads to victory. When we trust God's plan, even when it doesn't make sense, we experience His power in our lives.

In what areas of your life is God calling you to obedience, even when it seems difficult?

But Gideon told them, 'I will not rule over you, nor will my son rule over you. The Lord will rule over you.'
Judges 8:23

After Gideon's victory, the Israelites wanted to make him their king. But Gideon refused, reminding them that the Lord was their true ruler. Gideon showed humility, recognizing that his success was from God and that God alone deserved the glory.

Humility is an important part of our journey. When we achieve success, it's important to remember that it's not by our power but by God's grace.

How can you practice humility today, giving God the glory for your successes?

Gideon made the gold into an ephod, which he placed in Ophrah,
his town. All Israel prostituted themselves by worshiping it there,
and it became a snare to Gideon and his family.
Judges 8:27

Despite his earlier humility, Gideon made a mistake after his victory. He created an ephod out of gold, and it became an object of worship for the Israelites, leading them away from God. Even the best leaders can make mistakes, and those mistakes can have lasting consequences.

It's important to stay focused on God and avoid creating idols in our lives, even unintentionally. Our journey should always lead us closer to God, not away from Him.

Are there any areas in your life where you might
be creating idols, even unintentionally?

No sooner had Gideon died than the Israelites again prostituted
themselves to the Baals. They set up Baal-Berith as their god and
did not remember the Lord their God, who had rescued them from
the hands of all their enemies on every side.
Judges 8:33–34

After Gideon's death, the Israelites quickly fell back into idolatry. Without strong leadership and accountability, they forgot about the Lord and turned to other gods. This shows the importance of having accountability on our journey to help us stay focused on God.

We all need people in our lives who can help keep us on track, especially during difficult times. Accountability helps us remember God's faithfulness and stay committed to Him.

Who can you turn to for accountability in your journey with God?

*Again the Israelites cried out to the Lord, and he gave them a
deliverer—Ehud, a left-handed man, the son of Gera the Benjamite.*
Judges 3:15

Throughout the book of Judges, we see a pattern of the Israelites falling into sin, facing oppression, crying out to God, and God raising up a leader to deliver them. Ehud was one of those leaders, and he was an unlikely choice. He was left-handed, which was considered unusual, but God used him to deliver Israel from their enemies.

God often calls unexpected people to leadership. He looks beyond our abilities and sees our potential to serve Him. When God calls us, we should respond with courage, knowing that He will equip us for the task.

*Is there a leadership role God might be calling you to,
even if you feel unqualified?*

*Ehud reached with his left hand, drew the sword from his right
thigh, and plunged it into the king's belly.*
Judges 3:21

Ehud's left-handedness became a strategic advantage in his mission to deliver Israel. God used what others might see as a weakness and turned it into a strength. Ehud's courage and trust in God led to a great victory for Israel.

God can use our weaknesses for His glory. When we rely on Him, He can turn our shortcomings into strengths and accomplish great things through us.

How can you trust God to use your weaknesses for His purposes?

Now Deborah, a prophet, the wife of Lappidoth,
was leading Israel at that time.
Judges 4:4

Deborah was a remarkable leader in Israel. She was a prophet, a judge, and a military leader. Her wisdom and courage led Israel to victory over their enemies. Deborah's story shows that God can call anyone to leadership, regardless of gender or background.

God's calling is not limited by our circumstances. When He calls us to lead, He equips us with the wisdom and strength we need to fulfill His purposes.

What can you learn from Deborah's leadership about
following God's call in your own life?

DAY 328: BARAK'S FAITH

Barak said to her, 'If you go with me, I will go;
but if you don't go with me, I won't go.'
Judges 4:8

Barak was a military leader called by God to deliver Israel, but he was hesitant to go into battle without Deborah's presence. While his faith might have seemed weak, he still trusted God enough to follow His call, even if it meant relying on Deborah's support.

God understands our need for support and encouragement. He often provides us with companions on our journey who can strengthen our faith and help us fulfill His calling.

Who has God placed in your life to support and encourage you on your journey?

*On that day Deborah and Barak son of Abinoam sang this
song: 'When the princes in Israel take the lead, when the people
willingly offer themselves—praise the Lord!'*
Judges 5:1-2

After their victory, Deborah and Barak led the people in a song of worship and praise. They recognized that their victory was from the Lord and gave Him the glory. Worship is a powerful response to God's work in our lives. It acknowledges His power and reminds us of His faithfulness.

Worship should be a regular part of our journey with God. It keeps our focus on Him and strengthens our relationship with Him.

How can you incorporate worship into your daily journey with God?

*Jael went out to meet Sisera and said to him, 'Come, my lord,
come right in. Don't be afraid.' So he entered her tent, and she
covered him with a blanket.*
Judges 4:18

Jael was an unlikely hero in the story of Israel's victory over the Canaanites. She wasn't a warrior, but her quick thinking and courage led to the defeat of Israel's enemy, Sisera. Jael's actions remind us that God can use anyone to accomplish His purposes, even in unexpected ways.

God often works through ordinary people to do extraordinary things. When we trust Him and act in faith, He can use us in ways we never imagined.

How can you be open to God using you in unexpected ways?

In those days Israel had no king; everyone did as they saw fit.
Judges 17:6

Without strong, godly leadership, the Israelites fell into chaos and sin. The lack of a central leader led to a time of moral and spiritual decline in Israel. This verse highlights the importance of having leaders who follow God's ways and guide others to do the same.

Leadership is important in our journey with God. We need leaders who can guide us in truth and righteousness, helping us stay on the right path.

Who are the godly leaders in your life, and how can you support them?

Then Manoah prayed to the Lord: 'Pardon your servant, Lord.
I beg you to let the man of God you sent to us come again to teach
us how to bring up the boy who is to be born.'
Judges 13:8

Manoah, the father of Samson, prayed for guidance on how to raise his son, who would be set apart for God's purposes. This prayer shows humility and a desire to follow God's will, even in uncertainty.

God is merciful and provides guidance when we seek Him. Even when we don't have all the answers, He is willing to teach us and help us along the way.

How can you seek God's guidance in areas where you feel uncertain?

*Then the Spirit of the Lord came powerfully upon him. The ropes on his
arms became like charred flax, and the bindings dropped from his hands.*
Judges 15:14

Samson was known for his incredible physical strength, which was a gift
from God. However, despite his strength, Samson had weaknesses that ultimately led to his downfall. His story reminds us that our strengths come from
God, and we must rely on Him to use them wisely.

Our journey with God requires both strength and humility. We must recognize that our abilities are gifts from God and use them to serve Him rather
than relying on our power.

*How can you use your strengths to serve God while also
recognizing your need for His guidance?*

*Delilah said to Samson, 'Tell me the secret of your great strength
and how you can be tied up and subdued.'*
Judges 16:6

Samson's relationship with Delilah was filled with compromise. He allowed her to get close to him, even though she was working against him. This
compromise eventually led to his capture and loss of strength. Samson's story
warns us of the dangers of compromising our values and allowing others to
lead us away from God.

Our journey with God requires steadfastness and integrity. We must be
careful not to compromise our values or allow others to distract us from our
path.

*Are there areas in your life where you are tempted to compromise your values?
How can you stay strong in your commitment to God?*

But the hair on his head began to grow again after it had been shaved.
Judges 16:22

Even after Samson's fall, God wasn't finished with him. As his hair began to grow back, so did his strength. Samson's story shows that God offers redemption and second chances, even when we make mistakes.

No matter how far we've fallen, God is always ready to restore and use us again. His grace and mercy are greater than our failures.

How can you embrace God's grace and allow Him to restore you after a failure?

DAY 336: TRUSTING GOD IN THE DARK

Now Samuel died, and all Israel assembled and mourned for him;
and he was buried at his home in Ramah.
1 Samuel 25:1

Samuel was a prophet and judge who guided Israel faithfully. His death marked a significant loss for the people. During times of loss and darkness, it's important to trust that God is still in control and has a plan for our lives.

Even when we face difficult and dark times, God is with us. We can trust in His plan and seek His comfort and guidance.

How can you trust God during difficult and dark times in your life?

Give us a king to lead us." The people said to Samuel. "Now, this displeased Samuel; so he prayed to the Lord. And the Lord told him: 'Listen to all that the people are saying to you; it is not you they have rejected, but they have rejected me as their king.'
1 Samuel 8:6-7

The Israelites requested a king to lead them, which disappointed Samuel. Their request revealed a deeper issue: they were rejecting God's direct rule over them. This highlights the importance of recognizing God as our ultimate leader and guide.

In our journey, we may be tempted to seek other leaders or solutions, but we must remember that God is the true King who leads us with wisdom and love.

How can you ensure that God remains the ultimate leader in your life?

But the Lord said to Samuel, 'Do not consider his appearance or his height, for I have rejected him. The Lord does not look at the things people look at. People look at the outward appearance, but the Lord looks at the heart.'
1 Samuel 16:7

When Samuel was choosing a king, God reminded him that He looks at the heart, not outward appearances. David, the youngest and least likely of Jesse's sons, was chosen because of his heart for God.

God's choices often defy human expectations. When He calls us or others to serve, He looks at our hearts and our willingness to follow Him rather than our outward qualifications.

How can you focus on developing a heart that aligns with God's will?

*Saul was afraid of the people and their demands; he feared they
would leave him, so he offered the burnt offering himself.*
1 Samuel 13:12

King Saul's decision to offer the burnt offering himself instead of waiting for Samuel was a result of his fear and self-reliance. His actions showed a lack of trust in God's timing and instructions. This led to consequences for his reign.

Trusting God's timing and following His instructions is crucial in our journey. Self-reliance can lead us away from God's plan and cause us to act in ways that are not in line with His will.

*In what areas of your life are you tempted to rely
on yourself rather than trusting God?*

*But Samuel replied: 'Does the Lord delight in burnt offerings and
sacrifices as much as in obeying the Lord? To obey is better than
sacrifice, and to heed is better than the fat of rams.'*
1 Samuel 15:22

Samuel reminded Saul that obedience to God is more important than ritual sacrifices. God values our obedience and willingness to follow His commands above all else. Sacrifices without obedience are meaningless.

Obeying God's commands and following His guidance is essential in our journey. It shows our commitment to Him and our trust in His wisdom.

How can you practice obedience to God in your daily life?

Now the men of Judah had come to Hebron, and there they anointed David king over the tribe of Judah. When David was informed that it was the men of Jabesh Gilead who had buried Saul,
2 Samuel 2:4

David's anointing as king was marked by a time of fellowship and unity among the tribes of Israel. The people came together to support David and recognize God's choice for leadership. Fellowship and unity are important aspects of our journey with God.

Being part of a supportive and unified community strengthens our faith and helps us grow in our relationship with God. It's important to seek and value fellowship with other believers.

How can you cultivate meaningful fellowship with others in your faith community?

David inquired of the Lord, 'Shall I go up to one of the towns of Judah?' He answered, 'Go up.' David asked, 'Where shall I go?' 'To Hebron,' the Lord answered.
2 Samuel 2:1

David sought God's guidance through prayer before making decisions. His example shows the importance of seeking God's direction in all areas of our lives. Prayer is a powerful way to receive guidance and align our plans with God's will.

In our journey, seeking God's direction through prayer helps us stay on the right path and make decisions that honor Him.

How can you make prayer a regular part of your decision-making process?

When Abner son of Ner, the commander of Saul's army,
took Ish-bosheth son of Saul and brought him over to Mahanaim,
2 Samuel 2:8

Abner's actions in placing Ish-bosheth as king revealed the complexities of leadership and politics. Even amidst political maneuvers, integrity and faithfulness to God's will are crucial. Abner's choices had significant consequences for the nation.

Maintaining integrity in all areas of our lives ensures that we are living according to God's principles, even when facing challenging situations.

How can you maintain integrity in your decisions and actions?

David sent messengers to Ish-bosheth son of Saul, demanding his
wife Michal, whom he had married.
2 Samuel 3:13

David's request for Michal, Saul's daughter and his first wife, reflects the complexities of relationships and the need for forgiveness. Despite past conflicts, David sought to restore what was rightfully his, showing a willingness to mend broken relationships.

Forgiveness and reconciliation are important in our journey. They help restore relationships and bring healing where there has been hurt or division.

Is there someone you need to forgive or reconcile with in your life?

David danced before the Lord with all his might,
wearing a linen ephod.
2 Samuel 6:14

David's exuberant worship before the Lord demonstrated his deep joy and reverence for God. He celebrated God's presence with all his strength, showing that worship should be a wholehearted and joyful expression of our love for God.

Worship is an important part of our journey. It's a way to express our gratitude and delight in God, celebrating His goodness and faithfulness.

How can you express your joy and reverence for God through worship?

DAY 346: THE IMPORTANCE OF SEEKING GOD'S WILL

But what about the ark of God?' David asked.
'It has not been inquired of since Saul's time.'
2 Samuel 6:26

David's concern for the ark of God showed his desire to seek God's will and honor His presence. Even as he celebrated and led the people, he recognized the importance of inquiring about and following God's will.

Seeking God's will in all aspects of our lives ensures that we are aligned with His purpose and that our actions honor Him.

How can you seek God's will in your decisions and actions today?

*But when the time of the year came for kings to go off to war,
David sent Joab out with the king's men and the whole Israelite
army. They destroyed the Ammonites and besieged Rabbah. But
David remained in Jerusalem.*
2 Samuel 11:1

David's decision to stay in Jerusalem rather than go to war led to a series of events that ultimately resulted in sin and tragedy. This passage highlights the consequences of our choices and the importance of staying true to God's commands.

Our decisions have consequences, and it's important to follow God's guidance to avoid pitfalls and stay on the right path.

*How can you make choices that align with God's
commands and avoid negative consequences?*

*David said to Nathan, 'I have sinned against the Lord.' Nathan
replied, 'The Lord has taken away your sin. You are not going to die.'*
2 Samuel 12:13

David's repentance after his sin with Bathsheba was genuine and heartfelt. His acknowledgment of his wrongdoing and plea for forgiveness resulted in God's mercy. This passage shows the power of repentance and God's willingness to forgive.

Repentance restores our relationship with God and allows us to experience His forgiveness and grace.

How can you practice repentance and seek God's forgiveness in your life?

DAY 349: THE IMPORTANCE OF HUMILITY IN LEADERSHIP

But the king of the Ammonites died and his son
Hanun succeeded him as king.
2 Samuel 10:1

The transition of leadership in this passage illustrates the need for humility and trust in God, especially during times of change. Leaders must remain humble and rely on God's guidance to lead effectively and honor Him.

Humility is essential in leadership, as it allows us to serve others and follow God's guidance with the right heart.

How can you practice humility in your role as a leader?

DAY 350: THE POWER OF GENEROSITY

And the king said to the woman, 'What can I do for you?'
'Can I speak to you about a problem?' she replied.
2 Samuel 14:4

David's willingness to listen and offer help to the woman in need reflects the importance of generosity and compassion. Generosity extends beyond material gifts to include time, attention, and support for others.

Being generous in all aspects of our lives demonstrates God's love and kindness to those around us.

How can you show generosity and compassion to others in your daily life?

Then all the tribes of Israel came to David at Hebron and said,
'We are your own flesh and blood.'
2 Samuel 5:1

The unity of the tribes of Israel under David's leadership exemplifies the joy of community and shared purpose. Coming together as one people with a common goal strengthens our faith and enhances our ability to serve God.

Building a strong, supportive community is vital for our spiritual growth and for fulfilling God's mission.

How can you contribute to building a stronger community in your faith journey?

David replied to Araunah, 'No, I insist on paying you for it. I will not sacrifice to the Lord my God burnt offerings that cost me nothing.' So David bought the threshing floor and the oxen and paid fifty shekels of silver for them.
2 Samuel 24:24

David's insistence on paying for the offerings shows the importance of sacrifice and obedience to God. Offering something of value demonstrates our commitment and love for God.

Obedience often requires us to make personal sacrifices, showing that we value our relationship with God above all else.

What are some ways you can demonstrate your commitment to God through obedience and sacrifice?

Now the Lord had promised David that He would build a house
for him and his descendants.
2 Samuel 7:11

God's promise to David to establish his lineage and a house for him demonstrates the value of trusting in God's promises. God's promises are sure and provide hope and direction for our lives.

Trusting in God's promises gives us confidence and hope as we navigate life's challenges.

How can you hold onto and trust God's promises in your life?

I have sinned against the Lord,' David said. And Nathan replied,
'The Lord has taken away your sin. You are not going to die.'
2 Samuel 12:13

David's acknowledgment of his sin and request for forgiveness highlights the importance of seeking forgiveness and making things right with God. Genuine repentance leads to God's grace and restoration.

Seeking forgiveness and making amends is a vital part of maintaining the right relationship with God and others.

How can you seek forgiveness and make amends in your life today?

And the Lord was with David; he became more and more
powerful, because the Lord Almighty was with him.
2 Samuel 5:10

David's success and growth in power were a result of God's presence and blessing. When God is with us, we experience His support and guidance, which empowers us to achieve great things.

Recognizing and relying on God's presence in our lives strengthens us and helps us fulfill our purpose.

How can you invite and rely on God's presence in your daily life?

DAY 356: THE IMPORTANCE OF FOLLOWING GOD'S COMMANDS

So David did as the Lord commanded him, and he struck down
the Philistines all the way from Gibeon to Gezer.
2 Samuel 5:25

David's obedience to God's commands resulted in victory over his enemies. Following God's instructions leads to success and fulfillment of His plans for our lives.

Obedience to God's commands ensures that we align ourselves with His will and experience His blessings.

How can you ensure that you are following God's commands in your life?

David confessed to Nathan, 'I have sinned against the Lord.' Nathan replied, 'The Lord has taken away your sin. You are not going to die.
2 Samuel 12:13

David's repentance and confession were met with God's mercy. This shows that acknowledging our sins and seeking forgiveness leads to God's grace and restoration.

Repentance is a powerful step towards healing and renewal in our relationship with God.

How can you practice repentance and seek God's forgiveness in your life?

David became more and more powerful, because the Lord Almighty was with him.
2 Samuel 5:10

David's rise to power was marked by unity and alignment with God's will. Unity among God's people is crucial for achieving His purposes and experiencing His blessings.

Striving for unity in our relationships and communities helps us work together towards common goals and strengthens our collective faith.

How can you promote unity in your relationships and faith community?

DAY 359: THE JOY OF SERVING OTHERS

*David made a covenant with all the people of Israel on that day
at Hebron. They anointed David king over Israel.*
2 Samuel 5:3

David's service to the people and his role as king involved making a covenant and leading with humility and dedication. Serving others with a joyful heart reflects God's love and builds strong communities.

Serving others with joy and dedication honors God and fosters strong, supportive relationships.

How can you find joy in serving others in your daily life?

DAY 360: THE FAITHFULNESS OF GOD'S PROMISES

*The Lord had promised David that He would
build a house for him and his descendants.*
2 Samuel 7:11

God's promise to David reflects His faithfulness and commitment to fulfilling His word. Trusting in God's promises gives us hope and assurance in our journey.

God's faithfulness to His promises provides a foundation for our trust and hope in Him.

How can you rely on and trust God's promises in your life?

*'For the Lord your God is the one who goes with you to fight for
you against your enemies to give you victory.'*
Deuteronomy 20:4

God's guidance and presence are crucial for overcoming challenges and achieving victory. Seeking His direction ensures that we align with His will and receive His support.

Relying on God's guidance helps us navigate life's challenges and find success according to His plan.

How can you seek and follow God's guidance in your life?

*You have filled my heart with greater joy than when their grain
and new wine abound.*
Psalm 4:7

God's provision brings joy and fulfillment that surpasses material abundance. Recognizing and appreciating His provision enhances our gratitude and contentment.

Understanding the depth of God's provision enriches our sense of joy and gratitude.

How can you recognize and appreciate God's provision in your life?

The Lord is my shepherd, I lack nothing.
Psalm 23:1

God's presence as our shepherd provides for all our needs and ensures our well-being. Trusting in His guidance and care removes anxiety and instills peace.

Relying on God's presence and provision brings peace and assurance in our journey.

How can you trust in God's provision and presence in your daily life?

I will praise you, Lord, with all my heart;
I will tell of all your wonderful deeds.
Psalm 9:1

Worshiping God with all our hearts and recounting His deeds fills us with joy and gratitude. Worship is an expression of our love and appreciation for God's goodness.

Engaging in heartfelt worship strengthens our relationship with God and enhances our joy.

How can you incorporate worship into your daily life?

Salvation belongs to our God, who sits on the throne, and to the Lamb.
Revelation 7:10

God's salvation through Jesus Christ is the ultimate source of hope and assurance. Trusting in His salvation provides a foundation for our faith and a future filled with hope.

Embracing the hope of salvation gives us confidence and peace as we navigate life's journey.

How can you fully embrace the hope of God's salvation in your life?

9 789189 744813